FABULOUS FISH

FABULOUS FISH

SUSAN HICKS

NOTE

1. All recipes serve four unless otherwise stated.

2. All spoon measurements are level. Spoon measures can be bought in both imperial and metric sizes to give accurate measurement of small quantities.

3. All eggs are size 2 or 3 unless otherwise stated.

4. All sugar is granulated unless otherwise stated.

5. Preparation times are an average calculated during recipe testing.

6. Metric and imperial measurements have been calculated separately. Use one set of measurements only as they are not exact equivalents.

7. Cooking times may vary slightly depending on the individual oven. Dishes should be placed in the centre of an oven unless otherwise specified.

8. Always preheat the oven or grill to the specified temperature.

9. If using a fan-assisted oven, follow the manufacturer's instructions for guidance on temperature adjustments.

First published in Great Britain in 1989
This edition published in 1996 by Hamlyn
an imprint of Reed Consumer Books Limited
Michelin House, 81 Fulham Road, London SW3 6RB
and Auckland, Melbourne, Singapore and Toronto

CONTENTS

STARTERS

A seafood starter can set the scene for many a memorable meal and there is no reason why you should not continue the theme with the main course. Elaborate, though not complicated starters such as Layered Fish Terrine are enormously satisfying for the creative cook. A simple pâté on the other hand, can be a great ice-breaker at the start of a supper party, served with crisp crudités.

Dressed crab (see page 19)

LAYERED FISH TERRINE

SERVES 6-8

about 225 g (8 oz) large spinach leaves,
  trimmed and washed (or cabbage)
225 g (8 oz) firm-fleshed white fish fillets
  such as cod or coley, cut into bite-sized
  pieces
300 ml (½ pint) double cream
3 eggs
1 tablespoon chopped fennel leaves
salt
freshly ground black pepper
225 g (8 oz) fresh crab meat
pinch of cayenne
50 g (2 oz) pine nuts
a little butter

To garnish:
dill sprigs
pine nuts

Preparation time: 20 minutes
Cooking time: about 45 minutes
Oven: 160°C, 325°F, Gas Mark 3

Slices of this terrine are so pretty and impressive that you would think it had taken hours to prepare. In fact it is very simple. The resulting firm texture of this terrine is achieved by careful cooking, rather than by prolonged preparation. Fennel is not everyone's favourite flavour, so substitute dill – or a herb of your choice – if you wish.

1. Blanch the spinach leaves in boiling salted water for 2-3 minutes. Drain and pat dry with paper towels. Remove any coarse stalks or ribs from the spinach then set the leaves aside.
2. Process the fish, cream, eggs, fennel, salt and pepper in a food processor or blender until smooth, thick and mousse like; alternatively finely chop or mince the fish, whip the cream and combine the other ingredients with a fork until thick.
3. Season the crab meat with salt and pepper, add cayenne to taste, then add the pine nuts.
4. Grease a 1 kg (2 lb) loaf tin or terrine with the butter and carefully line with the spinach leaves, leaving enough overlap to fold over the top.
5. Spoon in half the white fish mixture, and cover with a layer of spinach leaves. Add the crab meat mixture, press down

lightly, follow with another layer of spinach, and complete the terrine by adding the remaining white fish mixture.
6. Fold over the overlapping spinach leaves to cover the top completely and place a sheet of greased greaseproof paper over the terrine.
7. Stand the loaf tin or terrine in a baking tin containing 5 cm (2 inches) boiling water, and bake in a preheated oven for about 45 minutes, or until the loaf is nice and firm to the touch.
8. When it has cooled slightly, invert the tin and turn out the terrine. Cool, then chill for several hours. Carefully slice the terrine, garnish with dill sprigs and pine nuts and serve with a salad.

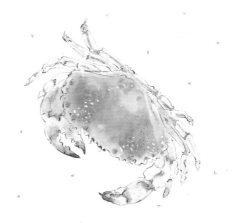

RIGHT: Layered fish terrine

TARAMASALATA

225 g (8 oz) smoked cod's roe
3 or 4 thick slices white bread, crusts
  removed
2 garlic cloves, crushed
300 ml (½ pint) olive oil
4 tablespoons fresh lemon juice
freshly ground black pepper
celery leaves, to garnish (optional)

To serve:
black olives
lemon wedges
toast triangles

Preparation time: 15 minutes, plus
soaking and chilling

True taramasalata is made from the smoked roe of the grey mullet, but smoked cod's roe is a good alternative.

1. Remove and discard the skin from the cod's roe and then soak the roe in water for 1 hour to reduce the saltiness.
2. Soak the slices of white bread in a bowl of cold water.
3. Drain the roe and pound with the garlic. Squeeze out the bread and add to the mixture, beating well.
4. Add the oil a little at a time, beating continuously, until the desired consistency is reached.
5. Add the lemon juice and season to taste with pepper.

6. Chill the taramasalata, garnish with celery leaves, if using, and serve with black olives, lemon wedges and toast triangles. Alternatively serve as a dip with raw celery and carrot sticks.

SEAFOOD PUFFS

MAKES ABOUT 18 PUFFS
2 tablespoons soured cream
1 teaspoon tomato purée
salt (optional)
freshly ground black pepper (optional)
1 smoked mackerel fillet or smoked salmon
  pieces
cayenne, to dust
salad leaves, to garnish

Choux pastry:
50 g (2 oz) butter
150 ml (¼ pint) water
25 g (1 oz) plain flour
25 g (1 oz) wholemeal flour
¼ teaspoon cayenne
2 eggs, beaten

Preparation time: 20 minutes
Cooking time: 25 minutes
Oven: 200°C, 400°F, Gas Mark 6

These are very light, and 2 or 3 on a plate with a salad garnish or small bunches of watercress and twists of lemon make a very attractive starter – they would also be good as part of a buffet lunch.

1. First make the choux pastry. Put the butter and water in a saucepan and bring to the boil. Remove from the heat and immediately beat in the flours and cayenne until the dough that forms leaves the side of the pan.
2. Let the mixture cool slightly, then gradually beat in the eggs a little at a time until the dough mixture is thoroughly amalgamated.
3. Place teaspoonfuls of the dough on a lightly greased baking tray, or alternatively pipe the dough, and bake in a preheated oven for about 20 minutes until well risen and firm to touch.
4. Transfer to a wire tray to cool.
5. Meanwhile, combine the soured cream and tomato purée to make a dressing –

taste and season lightly with salt and pepper if you wish.
6. Skin the mackerel or salmon and flake or cut into small strips.
7. Cut open each choux bun, fill with a little of the dressing, and top with flakes of the fish.
8. Serve on individual plates with a dusting of cayenne and a salad garnish.

ABOVE RIGHT: Taramasalata
BELOW RIGHT: Seafood puffs

SCALLOPS WITH TANGY ORANGE

8 prepared scallops
50 g (2 oz) butter
1 bunch spring onions, trimmed and finely
  chopped
juice of 1 orange
salt
freshly ground black pepper
2 teaspoons double cream or crème fraîche

To garnish:
orange twists
spring onion tassels

Preparation time: 10 minutes
Cooking time: 12 minutes

For a more substantial dish, serve the scallops on a bed of buttered noodles.

1. Remove the coral from the scallops and slice the white flesh.
2. Sauté the white and coral sections of the scallops in the butter for 2-3 minutes. Remove the scallops with a slotted spoon, and keep warm.
3. Put the spring onions into the pan and cook gently until soft.
4. Add the orange juice, season to taste with salt and pepper and stir well, taking up all the juices.
5. Remove from the heat and swirl in the cream or crème fraîche.

6. Arrange the scallops on individual plates or place into clean scallop shells and spoon over the sauce. Garnish with twists of orange and spring onion tassels.

FISH TARTLETS

MAKES ABOUT 8 TARTLETS
350 g (12 oz) cod fillet, cooked, skinned,
  and sliced into thin pieces
100 g (4 oz) soft goat's milk cheese
2 egg yolks, beaten
4 tablespoons single cream
2-3 teaspoons chopped fennel leaves

Shortcrust pastry:
50 g (2 oz) wholemeal flour
50 g (2 oz) plain flour
pinch of salt
50 g (2 oz) butter or margarine
1-2 tablespoons cold water

Preparation time: 25 minutes, plus
chilling and cooling
Cooking time: 20-25 minutes
Oven: 200°C, 400°F, Gas Mark 6

Use cod or any other firm white fish such as haddock or monkfish for these exquisitely flavoured little tartlets.

1. First make the pastry. Sift together the flours and salt. Rub in the butter or margarine until the mixture resembles fine breadcrumbs. Sprinkle over the water and bind the mixture together. Roll into a ball and chill for 20-30 minutes before using.
2. Roll out the chilled pastry and, using a pastry cutter, cut out about 8 rounds and use to line greased tartlet or bun tins. Press a square of foil into each and bake blind in a preheated oven for 10-12 minutes. Cool on a wire tray.
3. When cool, put a layer of cod into each tartlet. Combine the goat's milk cheese with the egg yolks, cream and chopped fennel, and top the fish with a spoonful of this mixture. Return to the oven for a further 10 minutes. Serve the fish tartlets either hot or cold with a colourful mixed salad.

ABOVE RIGHT: Scallops with tangy orange
BELOW RIGHT: Fish tartlets

SMOKED MACKEREL PATE

350 g (12 oz) smoked mackerel fillets
150 g (5 oz) low-fat cream cheese
2-3 teaspoons prepared horseradish sauce
2 tablespoons fresh lemon juice
freshly ground black pepper

To garnish:
lime wedges
rosemary sprigs

Preparation time: 15 minutes

1. Remove the skin and any bones from the fish, then flake into a bowl. Add the cream cheese and horseradish sauce, and mix together thoroughly until well combined.
2. Add the fresh lemon juice and black pepper, tasting until the desired piquancy is achieved.
3. Garnish with lime wedges and sprigs of rosemary and serve with a salad and triangles of Melba toast.

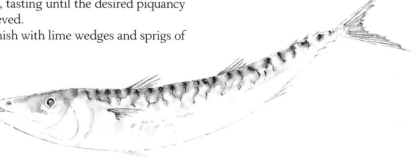

PRAWNS WITH GARLIC

SERVES 4-6
50 g (2 oz) butter
1 small onion, peeled and finely chopped
2 large garlic cloves, peeled and finely
  chopped
1 red pepper, cored, seeded and chopped
450 g (1 lb) peeled cooked prawns or sliced
  Dublin Bay prawns (scampi)
1 tablespoon lemon juice
salt
freshly ground black pepper
chopped parsley

To garnish:
whole, cooked, unpeeled prawns
basil sprigs

Preparation time: 10 minutes
Cooking time: 8-9 minutes

ABOVE LEFT: Smoked mackerel pâté
BELOW LEFT: Prawns with garlic

1. In a heavy frying or sauté pan, melt the butter and gently cook the onion, garlic and red pepper until soft but not browned.
2. Turn up the heat slightly, and add the prawns, mix well and sauté for 2-3 minutes. If using scampi, cook for 4-5 minutes.

3. Add the lemon juice, season to taste with salt and pepper and sprinkle over the chopped parsley.
4. Garnish with a whole, cooked, unpeeled prawn and sprigs of basil. Serve immediately with a green salad and crusty bread to mop up the tasty garlic juices.

CRAB AND AVOCADO MOUSSE

SERVES 6-8
2 ripe avocados
4 tablespoons soured cream
350 g (12 oz) fresh white crab meat, flaked
pinch of salt
pinch of white pepper
squeeze of fresh lemon juice
20 g (¾ oz) powdered gelatine
6 tablespoons hot water
2 egg whites, lightly whisked
basil sprigs, to garnish

To serve:
1 radicchio, shredded
20 radishes, sliced
3-4 tablespoons cocktail sauce (see page 140)

Preparation time: 25 minutes, plus chilling

This delicately flavoured and coloured mousse needs to be served as soon as it has chilled and set as the avocado will lose its colour and flavour if kept for much longer than this. I like to use a melon baller or teaspoon when serving the mousse – the pale green mousse balls set on individual plates with a garnish of salad are most impressive.

1. Cut the avocados in half lengthways and remove the stones. Scoop out the flesh, chop roughly and place in a food processor or liquidiser with the soured cream and crab meat then blend until smooth.
2. Season to taste with salt, pepper and a squeeze of lemon juice, then transfer to a large glass or china bowl.
3. Dissolve the gelatine in the hot water and allow to cool before stirring into the crab and avocado mixture. Put in the refrigerator until nearly set (about 30 minutes-1 hour), then fold in the whisked egg whites.
4. Return the mousse to the refrigerator for about 2 hours, or until set.
5. Use a melon baller or teaspoon to scoop the mousse on to a bed of the radicchio and sliced radishes and pour a little cocktail sauce over the mousse. Garnish with sprigs of basil.

MOULES A LA MARINIERE

SERVES 4-6
3.5 litres (6 pints) mussels
25 g (1 oz) butter
1 onion, peeled and finely chopped
300 ml (½ pint) dry white wine
1 bay leaf
3 thyme sprigs
3 tablespoons chopped parsley
salt
freshly ground black pepper

To garnish:
1-2 tablespoons chopped parsley
bay leaves
parsley sprigs

Preparation time: 20 minutes
Cooking time: 15-20 minutes

1. Scrub and clean the mussels, removing any beards (see page 137). Discard any mussels which are open and do not close when lightly tapped.
2. Melt the butter over a gentle heat and add the onion. Cook for a few minutes until softened then add the wine, bay leaf, thyme and parsley. Season with pepper and bring to the boil.
3. Place the mussels in this liquid and cook for about 5-10 minutes, or until the shells are open. It is important to remember to discard any mussels which have not opened during cooking.
4. Remove the open mussels with a slotted spoon and keep warm.
5. Strain the cooking liquid and season with salt and pepper to taste. Pour the strained liquid over the mussels.
6. Garnish with chopped parsley, bay leaves and sprigs of parsley.

ABOVE RIGHT: Crab and avocado mousse
BELOW RIGHT: Moules à la marinière

DRESSED CRAB

SERVES 4-6
2 cooked crabs, about 750 g (1½ lb) each
salt
freshly ground black pepper
2 hard-boiled eggs
4 tablespoons finely chopped parsley
paprika
a few drops of lemon juice

To serve (optional):
a selection of salad leaves
mayonnaise (see page 140)
lemon wedges
brown bread and butter

Preparation time: 40 minutes

Preparing a dressed crab is well worth while – there is no mystique about it and the result is pretty and impressive.

1. Extract the white and brown meat from the crabs as explained on page 137 and keep them separate.
2. Tap out the shell of the crab as described on page 137 then wash thoroughly in boiling water and dry with paper towels.
3. Lightly season the crab meat with salt and pepper.
4. Separate the yolk and white of the hard-boiled eggs and push through a sieve.
5. Arrange the brown crab meat down the sides of each shell then place a strip of sieved hard-boiled egg white on top of them. Make a similar strip of chopped parsley followed by the sieved egg yolk.
6. Heap the white crab meat in the centre of the shells and sprinkle with a little lemon juice. Top with sieved egg white.
7. Sprinkle the paprika in a line down between the egg yolk and the egg white.
8. Set the dressed crabs on a platter of salad leaves and serve with mayonnaise, wedges of lemon and thin slices of brown bread and butter.

GRILLED OYSTERS WITH GARLIC BUTTER

16 oysters, scrubbed
16 thick slices bread (optional)
100 g (4 oz) butter, softened
2 garlic cloves, crushed
2-4 tablespoons roughly chopped parsley
fresh wholemeal breadcrumbs
3 tablespoons freshly grated Parmesan
  cheese (optional)

To serve:
lemon wedges
brown bread and butter

Preparation time: 20 minutes
Cooking time: 2 minutes

ABOVE LEFT: Dressed crab
BELOW LEFT: Grilled oysters with garlic butter

The romantic and luxurious image of oysters was not always so – they were once the food of the poor. Now, with exciting developments in their production and distribution, they are within the scope of the average household purse again. This way of serving them hot is simple and highly recommended – especially with a glass of champagne at hand!

1. First open the oysters (see page 138).
2. Return the oysters to the deeper rounded shell and arrange in a baking dish – taking care not to spill the juice. To keep the oysters upright you could stand them in thick slices of bread in which you have cut out round shapes to cradle the shells and keep them steady.
3. Cream the butter and garlic together, add the parsley and beat in. Put a knob of this butter on each oyster, then a good sprinkling of breadcrumbs. Dot a few tiny pieces of the garlic butter over the bread-crumbs and, if you like, a sprinkling of Parmesan cheese.
4. Grill for no more than 2 minutes.
5. Serve immediately, with lemon wedges and triangles of brown bread and butter to mop up the lovely juices.

SIMPLE SARDINES

SERVES 4-6
12 fresh sardines
225 g (8 oz) ricotta cheese
salt
freshly ground black pepper

To garnish (optional):
thyme sprigs
feverfew sprigs

To serve:
lemon wedges
brown bread and butter

Preparation time: 20 minutes
Cooking time: 6-8 minutes

1. Remove the heads from the sardines and discard. Split down the belly of the sardine and clean well.
2. Turn the sardine over and press down the backbone, turn over again so that the skin is face down and carefully remove the backbone.
3. Spread each sardine with a generous amount of ricotta cheese, season to taste with salt and pepper and roll up the sardines from head to tail.
4. Cook under a preheated hot grill – or barbecue for 3-4 minutes each side.
5. Garnish with sprigs of thyme and feverfew, if using, and serve with wedges of lemon and brown bread and butter.

COQUILLES SAINT JACQUES

8 prepared scallops, halved
300 ml (½ pint) milk
salt
freshly ground black pepper
50 g (2 oz) butter
50 g (2 oz) mushrooms, wiped and thinly
  sliced
25 g (1 oz) plain flour
1 tablespoon dry sherry
50 g (2 oz) fresh white breadcrumbs
50 g (2 oz) Cheshire cheese, grated
½ teaspoon dried mustard powder

To garnish (optional):
lemon twists
rue sprigs
chives

Preparation time: 15 minutes
Cooking time: 12-15 minutes

1. Gently poach the scallops in the milk seasoned with salt and pepper for about 4 minutes. Drain and reserve the stock.
2. Melt the butter in a pan and sauté the mushrooms for 2 minutes. Stir in the flour and cook for a few minutes. Gradually add the reserved stock (made up to 300 ml (½ pint) with more milk if necessary). Bring to the boil, stirring continuously.
3. Stir in the scallops and sherry and spoon the mixture into small dishes or cleaned scallop shells if you have them.
4. Mix the breadcrumbs, cheese and mustard powder together and sprinkle over the scallop mixture.
5. Place under a moderate grill until golden brown and bubbling. Garnish with lemon twists, rue sprigs and chives, if using, then serve.

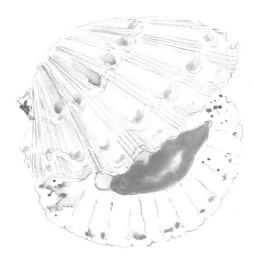

ABOVE RIGHT: Simple sardines
BELOW RIGHT: Coquilles Saint Jacques

SOUPS

Some fish soups are so packed full of ingredients that they are a meal in themselves; the classic Bouillabaisse is a good example. Others can be smooth, fragrant and delicate, such as Lobster Bisque, providing a stunning introduction to a dinner party. Experiment with vegetables and herbs in season to create your own soups, chowders and bisques. There is enormous scope for your own personal touch.

Prawn and sweetcorn chowder (see page 31)

BOUILLABAISSE

SERVES 8-10

1 kg (2 lb) mixed fish and shellfish (such as firm-fleshed cod, haddock, whiting, coley, John Dory, mussels, peeled cooked prawns or shrimps)
3 tablespoons olive oil
2 onions, peeled and chopped
2-3 garlic cloves, crushed
2 celery sticks, trimmed and thinly sliced
3 potatoes, peeled and thinly sliced
450 g (1 lb) tomatoes, peeled and chopped
bouquet garni of 2 bay leaves, thyme and parsley
2 strips orange rind
pinch of saffron strands or 1 teaspoon saffron powder infused in 600 ml (1 pint) fish stock or warm water
salt
freshly ground black pepper
aïoli (see page 141), to serve
1-2 tablespoons chopped parsley, to garnish

Preparation time: 25 minutes
Cooking time: 30-35 minutes

This is a great French Mediterranean classic. Like the Spanish paella, there are many versions and variations – so that it offers great scope to the keen and imaginative cook. It is filling and rich and can be offered as a hearty main course. Ideally use Mediterranean fish according to season and availability – and choose inexpensive shellfish such as mussels or whatever your fishmonger recommends as a good buy. Whatever combination of ingredients you use, bouillabaisse should always include saffron, garlic, olive oil and tomatoes.

1. Scale, clean and cut the fish into fairly thick pieces (see page 134).
2. Heat the olive oil in a large, heavy pan and soften the onions and garlic. Add the celery and potatoes and continue cooking for 1-2 minutes.
3. Slide in the chopped tomatoes, herbs, orange rind and pour in the infused water. Season with salt and pepper and bring to the boil. Add the firmer-fleshed white fish and simmer – do not boil – for 5 minutes.
4. Scrub the mussels and remove the beards. Add them to the pan with any other soft-fleshed fish and prawns if using. Just cook gently and briefly until all the fish and shellfish are cooked but firm, remembering to discard any mussels that do not open, if using.
5. Transfer the bouillabaisse to a soup tureen, stir in the aïoli, garnish with parsley and serve with hot garlic bread or croûtons.

RIGHT: Bouillabaisse

LOBSTER BISQUE

75 g (3 oz) butter
2 medium carrots, scraped and roughly chopped
1 celery stick, trimmed and chopped
1 onion, peeled and roughly chopped
1 lobster or crawfish shell, legs and any scraps of left-over flesh
6 black peppercorns
pinch of salt
1 small bunch parsley
50 g (2 oz) plain flour
2 teaspoons coarsely chopped mint
150 ml (¼ pint) double cream

Preparation time: 15 minutes, plus chilling
Cooking time: about 40-45 minutes

Having splashed out on lobster or crawfish – and thoroughly enjoyed it – you will be delighted to know that there is yet more to come! The pounded shells of these shellfish can produce a lovely stock, from which I have devised this extremely elegant soup.

1. In a large, heavy saucepan, melt 25 g (1 oz) of the butter and sweat the prepared vegetables for 5-7 minutes.
2. Break up the shells and legs of the lobster or crawfish and pack on top of the vegetables. Just cover with water and add the peppercorns, salt and parsley. Gently simmer for 30-45 minutes.
3. Strain this stock through a sieve into a bowl and reserve.

4. Melt the remaining butter in a pan, stir in the flour and cook for a few minutes. Remove from the heat and gradually add the reserved stock. Return to the heat and bring to the boil, stirring all the time, then taste and adjust the seasoning if necessary. Simmer for 5-6 minutes then add the chopped mint and stir in the double cream. Add also any reserved flakes of shellfish flesh if you have them.
5. Heat through and serve with warmed French bread.

GENOESE FISH SOUP

SERVES 4-6
25 g (1 oz) butter
1 onion, peeled and chopped
3 sticks celery, trimmed and sliced
50 g (2 oz) rindless streaky bacon, chopped
1×400 g (14 oz) can chopped tomatoes
150 ml (¼ pint) dry white wine
300 ml (½ pint) fish stock (see page 139)
½ teaspoon marjoram
salt
freshly ground black pepper
450 g (1 lb) monkfish, cod or coley, boned, skinned and diced
100 g (4 oz) peeled cooked prawns
2 tablespoons chopped parsley, to garnish

Preparation time: 20 minutes
Cooking time: 25-30 minutes

1. Melt the butter in a large saucepan and soften the onion for 2-3 minutes.
2. Add the celery and bacon to the pan and continue cooking over a low heat for a few more minutes.
3. Add the tomatoes, wine, stock, marjoram and season with salt and pepper. Simmer for 10 minutes.
4. Add the fish and cook for 5 minutes.
5. Finally add the prawns and simmer for a further 2-3 minutes. Taste and adjust the seasoning, if necessary, and serve hot with warmed rolls, garnished with chopped parsley.

ABOVE LEFT: Lobster bisque
BELOW LEFT: Genoese fish soup

Garlic lovers can add a clove of garlic to this tasty soup to give extra flavour. Add the crushed or finely chopped clove of garlic to the saucepan of melted butter together with the chopped onion then continue the recipe as instructed.

MUSSEL AND TOMATO SOUP

SERVES 4-6

1 large onion, peeled and chopped
4 tablespoons olive oil
1×400 g (14 oz) can chopped tomatoes
300 ml (½ pint) dry white wine
1 teaspoon oregano
salt
freshly ground black pepper
2.25 litres (4 pints) mussels
2 tablespoons double cream
2 tablespoons chopped parsley, to garnish

Preparation time: 20 minutes
Cooking time: about 25 minutes

You can add a couple of tablespoons of freshly grated Parmesan cheese to this simple, earthy soup, if you wish.

1. Soften the onion in the olive oil then add the tomatoes, wine, oregano and season with salt and pepper to taste. Simmer for about 10 minutes.
2. Meanwhile, scrub the mussels and remove the beards, discard any which are open and do not close when lightly tapped. Put the mussels into the soup and let them gently steam open. Remember to discard any mussels which do not open during cooking.
3. After a few minutes, stir in the double cream and add a little more wine or some fish stock if the soup is too thick.
4. Serve in large soup bowls garnished with chopped parsley. Use the halved mussel shells to scoop up the soup and mop up the juices with warm fresh bread.

HEARTY FISH SOUP

SERVES 6

2 tablespoons olive oil
3-4 garlic cloves, crushed
2 large onions, peeled and chopped
2 leeks, washed, trimmed and sliced
2 large carrots, scraped and thinly sliced
1×400 g (14 oz) can chopped tomatoes
900 ml (1½ pints) fish stock (see page 139)
300 ml (½ pint) white wine
bouquet garni of bay leaf, parsley and
  thyme
juice and rind of 1 orange
salt
freshly ground black pepper
1 kg (2 lb) assorted mixed fish or fish fillets,
  according to season
thyme sprigs, to garnish

Preparation time: 20 minutes
Cooking time: 25-35 minutes

This soup can be prepared in advance up to the stage where the fish is added.

1. Heat the olive oil in a large, deep, heavy saucepan and soften the garlic and onion.
2. Add the leeks and carrots and cook for 1-2 minutes.
3. Tip in the tomatoes, stock, wine, herbs, orange juice and rind. Season to taste with salt and pepper, bring to the boil, reduce the heat and simmer for about 15 minutes.
4. Meanwhile, clean and prepare the fish, and cut into bite-sized pieces. Add the firm white fish and cook for 3-4 minutes, then add the softer-fleshed fish and cook for a further 2 or 3 minutes.
5. Pour the soup into a warmed tureen or individual soup bowls and garnish with sprigs of thyme.

ABOVE RIGHT: Mussel and tomato soup
BELOW RIGHT: Hearty fish soup

CHILLED AVOCADO AND SMOKED HADDOCK SOUP

SERVES 3-4
450 g (1 lb) smoked haddock fillets
600 ml (1 pint) milk, lemon and herb stock (see page 139)
2 ripe avocados
about 300 ml (½ pint) fish stock (see page 139)
salt
freshly ground black pepper
1 tablespoon plain unsweetened yogurt (optional)
mint leaves, to garnish (optional)

Preparation time: 20 minutes, plus chilling
Cooking time: 5 minutes

1. Gently poach the smoked haddock fillets in the milk stock for about 5 minutes, using just enough to cover the fillets. Remove from the heat and allow to cool. Reserve the poaching liquid and strain through a sieve.
2. Skin the haddock fillets and flake the flesh roughly.
3. Halve the avocados, remove the stones, peel off the skin and chop the flesh. Put into a food processor or liquidiser with the reserved poaching liquid and the flaked haddock. Blend until smooth then transfer to a large glass or china bowl.
4. With a balloon whisk, stir in sufficient fish stock to thin down the mixture to a creamy consistency. Taste and season with salt and pepper, and add the yogurt at this stage, if using.
5. Chill the soup before serving. Do not keep this soup for too long before serving as the avocados tend to lose their colour and flavour.
6. Garnish the individual bowls of chilled soup with whole mint leaves, if using, and serve with chilled white wine and crusty rolls.

PRAWN AND SWEETCORN CHOWDER

SERVES 4-6
1 large onion, peeled and chopped
1 green pepper, cored, seeded and chopped
2 tablespoons oil
450 g (1 lb) potatoes, peeled and diced
900 ml (1½ pints) fish stock (see page 139)
350 g (12 oz) white fish, skinned and cut into bite-sized pieces
225 g (8 oz) peeled cooked prawns
225 g (8 oz) sweetcorn
salt
freshly ground black pepper
1-2 tablespoons chopped parsley, to garnish

Preparation time: 20 minutes
Cooking time: about 25 minutes

Use any firm-fleshed white fish, such as cod, coley, haddock or monkfish for this filling soup.

1. Soften the chopped onion and green pepper in the oil for a few minutes, then add the potatoes.
2. Pour in the stock and simmer gently for 10 minutes.
3. Add the fish and cook for 5 minutes, then add the prawns and sweetcorn and continue cooking for 3-4 minutes.
4. Season to taste with salt and pepper and garnish with the chopped parsley.

ABOVE LEFT: Chilled avocado and smoked haddock soup
BELOW LEFT: Prawn and sweetcorn chowder

LA BOURRIDE

SERVES 8

2 leeks, washed, trimmed and finely sliced
1 onion, peeled and finely sliced
3 garlic cloves
450 g (1 lb) potatoes, sliced
1.5 kg (3 lb) firm white fish, filleted and cut
  into bite-sized pieces
½ quantity aïoli (see page 141)
olive oil, for frying
1 stick French bread, thickly sliced

Stock:
225 g (8 oz) white fish trimmings
2 onions, peeled and chopped
2-3 celery sticks, trimmed and chopped
salt
freshly ground black pepper

Preparation time: 35 minutes
Cooking time: about 1 hour

A classic Provençal fish soup with garlic – certainly hearty enough for a main meal. The preparation is rather time consuming but is well worth the effort. You can use your own choice and combination of fish – I recommend monkfish, perhaps some fillet of turbot – or haddock, cod and halibut. There are many different versions of this soup; this is mine.

1. First, make the stock. Put all the ingredients into a large saucepan and season with salt and pepper. Bring to the boil, reduce the heat and simmer for 30 minutes, skimming off the scum that rises to the surface from time to time. Strain the stock through a wire sieve.
2. Put the leeks, onion, 2 cloves of crushed garlic and the potatoes in a large pan and place the fish on top. Cover with the strained stock, and poach for about 10 minutes or until the fish is tender. Keep an eye on the fish as different varieties and thicknesses cook at different speeds – be careful not to let it overcook and break up.
3. With a slotted spoon or fish slice, transfer the cooked fish and potatoes to a

heated dish and keep warm.
4. Reduce the remaining stock in the pan down to one third of the quantity, let it cool slightly, then strain slowly and carefully into the aïoli, beating all the time. Then gently heat this soup in a saucepan, but do not allow it to boil.
5. Rub the inside of a frying pan with the remaining clove of garlic, and heat up the olive oil. Fry the slices of French bread in the oil and place a slice in the bottom of individual soup bowls. Place the reserved fish and potatoes on top and ladle over the soup. Serve immediately.

RIGHT: La bourride

FISHERMAN'S CHOWDER

SERVES 6

50 g (2 oz) butter
1 large onion, peeled and thinly sliced
100 g (4 oz) rindless bacon, chopped
4 celery sticks, trimmed and chopped
1 small red or green pepper, cored, seeded
  and diced
1 large potato, peeled and diced
300 ml (½ pint) fish stock (see page 139)
750 g (1½ lb) smoked and white fish (such
  as cod, coley, smoked haddock), skinned
  and cubed
300 ml (½ pint) milk
1 tablespoon cornflour
salt
freshly ground black pepper

Preparation time: 20 minutes
Cooking time: about 35 minutes

1. Melt the butter in a large saucepan. Cook the onion, bacon, celery, pepper and potato for 5 minutes.
2. Add the stock and simmer until the potatoes are just tender then add the fish to the pan.

3. Blend the milk and cornflour together, then stir into the pan, bring to the boil, stirring occasionally, reduce the heat and simmer for 5 minutes.
4. Season with salt and pepper to taste before serving.

COD AND KIPPER CHOWDER

SERVES 6

25 g (1 oz) butter
1 medium onion, peeled and finely chopped
600 ml (1 pint) fish stock (see page 139)
600 ml (1 pint) milk
2-3 potatoes, scrubbed and diced
275 g (10 oz) cod fillet, skinned and cut
  into small, bite-sized pieces
275 g (10 oz) kipper fillet, skinned and cut
  into small, bite-sized pieces
100 g (4 oz) peeled cooked prawns
  (optional)
squeeze of fresh lemon juice
freshly ground black pepper

Preparation time: 25 minutes
Cooking time: 25-30 minutes

ABOVE LEFT: Fisherman's chowder
BELOW LEFT: Cod and kipper chowder

This is a delicious soup, and I like to add some prawns in the finishing stages to enhance the lovely fresh seafish taste.

1. Melt the butter in a large heavy pan over a gentle heat and slowly sweat the onion until pale and soft.
2. Add the stock and milk and bring up to just gentle simmering point, then add the diced potato. Simmer for about 5-8 minutes, until the potato is half cooked, then add the pieces of cod and continue to cook for a further 2-3 minutes.
3. Add the kipper, prawns, if using, and continue to cook gently until they are heated through. Check the seasoning. The kipper and your fish stock should make the need for further salt unnecessary, but you can add a squeeze of lemon juice and a sprinkle of pepper to taste. Serve with warm bread rolls.

Kippers are made from good quality fresh herring. The herring are split and gutted, usually by machine, then soaked in brine, dyes may be added to the solution at this point. The fish are then hung up for 1 hour before being smoked.

EVERYDAY DISHES

Fish and shellfish has a great deal to offer to the imaginative and busy cook. This chapter contains many family favourites including Crispy Fish Hotpot, together with a selection of tasty new ideas such as Huss with Almonds and Apple. Be adventurous and substitute species of fish according to the season and availability.

Smoked mackerel with stir-fried vegetables (see page 46)

CHILLED MARINATED COD STEAKS

4 cod steaks
a little oil

Marinade:
150 ml (¼ pint) dry white wine
2 garlic cloves, crushed
12 cloves
juice and rind of 2 oranges and 2 lemons
bouquet garni of parsley, tarragon, thyme
  and bay leaf
salt
freshly ground black pepper

To garnish:
a selection of fresh herbs
lemon twists
orange twists

Preparation time: 15 minutes, plus
chilling overnight
Cooking time: about 15 minutes

1. Gently fry the cod steaks in a little oil for a few minutes on each side. Carefully lift them out of the pan with a fish slice and arrange on the base of a dish suitable to hold the marinade.
2. Make up the marinade with the listed ingredients and pour into the fish juices in the pan. Stir as you bring the marinade up to the boil then simmer for 5 minutes to extract the aroma and flavour of the herbs and spices.
3. Carefully pour the marinade over the cod steaks to cover completely. Leave to cool, cover with foil or clingfilm, then refrigerate overnight.
4. To serve, lift the cod steaks on to a dish, carefully remove and discard the skin and central bone and separate the flakes of fish. Strain the marinade and pour it over the fish steaks. Garnish the marinated cod with a selection of fresh herbs and twists of lemon and orange.

COD STEAKS A LA GRECQUE

1 onion, peeled and finely chopped
1 garlic clove, crushed
a little olive oil
50 g (2 oz) tomato purée
150 ml (¼ pint) fish stock (see page 139)
6 green and 6 black olives, pitted
2 tablespoons dry sherry
salt
freshly ground black pepper
4 cod steaks

To garnish:
fennel sprigs
celery leaves

Preparation time: 15 minutes
Cooking time: 30-35 minutes
Oven: 180°C, 350°F, Gas Mark 4

1. Gently cook the onion and garlic in a little olive oil until transparent, but do not let it brown.
2. Add the tomato purée, fish stock, green and black olives, sherry and season with salt and pepper to taste.
3. Arrange the cod steaks in a lightly greased ovenproof dish, and pour the sauce over and around them. Bake in a preheated oven for 20-25 minutes.
4. Garnish with fennel sprigs and celery leaves and serve immediately with a selection of green vegetables.

FAR RIGHT: Chilled marinated cod steaks
RIGHT: Cod steaks à la grecque

SEAFISH AUBERGINES

2 medium or 4 small aubergines
salt
freshly ground black pepper
450 g (1 lb) coley fillets
50 g (2 oz) butter
4 tablespoons fresh lemon juice
2 courgettes, diced
1 onion, peeled and chopped
2 garlic cloves, crushed
1 tablespoon oil
225 g (8 oz) tomatoes, peeled and chopped
1 teaspoon oregano or basil
100 g (4 oz) Cheddar or Gruyère cheese,
  grated
oregano sprigs, to garnish

Preparation time: 20 minutes, plus
removing the juices from the aubergines
Cooking time: about 1 hour 20 minutes
Oven: 180°C, 350°F, Gas Mark 4; then:
200°C, 400°F, Gas Mark 6; then: 220°C,
425°F, Gas Mark 7

Any firm white fish such as cod, haddock
and monkfish may be used for this dish.

1. Cut the aubergines in half lengthways,
score the flesh, sprinkle with salt and
leave to draw out the bitter juices for
30 minutes.
2. Meanwhile, season the fish fillets with
salt and pepper, dot with a little butter,
squeeze over a little lemon juice and wrap
in foil. Bake in a preheated oven for
15-20 minutes until cooked.
3. Wash the salt off the aubergines and pat
dry with paper towels. Place, flesh side
down, on a lightly greased baking dish
and bake in a preheated oven for about
40 minutes, until the flesh is tender. Allow
to cool slightly, then run a sharp knife
around the edge of the flesh and skin and
scoop out the flesh.
4. Put the aubergine flesh into a mixing
bowl and chop, then mash with a fork.

5. Soften the courgette, onion and garlic in
the remaining butter and the oil.
6. Add the chopped tomatoes to the
aubergine, and stir in the courgette
mixture, the oregano or basil and the
flaked coley, season with salt and pepper
and pile the mixture back into the
aubergine shells. Top with the grated
cheese and bake in a preheated oven for
10-15 minutes, until brown and bubbling.
7. Garnish with sprigs of oregano.

MEDITERRANEAN-STYLE COLEY

1 onion, peeled and chopped
1 garlic clove, crushed
25 g (1 oz) butter, melted
2 tomatoes, peeled, seeded and roughly
  chopped
225 g (8 oz) courgettes, sliced
1 tablespoon tomato purée
1 teaspoon fresh marjoram
pinch of salt
pinch of freshly ground black pepper
750 g (1½ lb) coley fillets, skinned and cut
  into bite-sized pieces

Preparation time: 20 minutes
Cooking time: 25-30 minutes

You could also use cod or huss for this
quick and simple dish.

1. Cook the onion and garlic gently in the
butter for a few minutes until pale in
colour and soft.
2. Mix in all the ingredients except the
coley and cook gently for 10-15 minutes,

until the courgettes are tender. Then add
the coley, and continue cooking for a
further 10 minutes.
3. Serve immediately, accompanied by
parsleyed rice.

ABOVE LEFT: Seafish aubergines
BELOW LEFT: Mediterranean-style coley

HAKE FLORENTINE

75 g (3 oz) butter
4 hake cutlets
salt
freshly ground black pepper
squeeze of fresh lemon juice
750 g (1½ lb) spinach
1 onion, peeled and finely chopped
1 garlic clove, crushed
25 g (1 oz) wholemeal flour
300 ml (½ pint) skimmed milk
2 tomatoes, sliced
100 g (4 oz) Gruyère cheese, grated
paprika
chervil sprigs, to garnish (optional)

Preparation time: 25 minutes
Cooking time: 40-45 minutes
Oven: 180°C, 350°F, Gas Mark 4; then:
220°C, 425°F, Gas Mark 7

This dish would be equally delicious if made with cutlets of other varieties of firm-fleshed white fish, such as cod or haddock.

1. Lightly butter a sheet of foil. Season the hake cutlets with salt and pepper, sprinkle with lemon juice and top with a few knobs of butter. Place in the foil and wrap up.
2. Put the foil parcel onto a baking sheet and bake in a preheated oven for 20 minutes or until just tender.
3. Cook the spinach in boiling, salted water for 3-4 minutes then drain and squeeze out all the moisture. Chop finely.
4. Melt 25 g (1 oz) of the butter and gently cook the onion and garlic. Cool slightly and mix into the finely chopped spinach.
5. Make the sauce. Melt the remaining 25 g (1 oz) butter in a saucepan, add the flour and stir continuously for 2 minutes over a low heat. Remove the pan from the heat and gradually add the milk and salt and pepper to taste, stirring all the time, any juices from the cooked cutlets can also be added. Return the pan to a low heat, bring to the boil and cook for 2-3 minutes, stirring constantly until the sauce thickens.
6. Make a base of spinach in a lightly greased ovenproof dish and make 4 dents in this base in which to place the cutlets.
7. Cover with the sauce and make an overlapping line of sliced tomatoes over the dish. Top with the grated cheese and a sprinkling of paprika then brown under a grill or bake in a hot oven for 8-10 minutes until golden and bubbling.
8. Garnish with sprigs of chervil, if using.

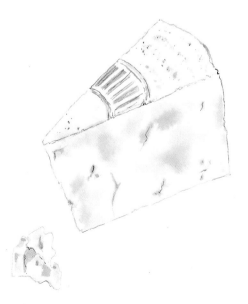

RIGHT: Hake florentine

MACKEREL WITH LEMON AND ROSEMARY

4 mackerel
4 sprigs fresh or 2 teaspoons dried rosemary
salt
freshly ground black pepper
juice and rind of 2-3 lemons
50 g (2 oz) butter or 2 tablespoons oil

To garnish:
rosemary sprigs
lemon slices

Preparation time: 20 minutes
Cooking time: 15-20 minutes

1. Clean the mackerel (see page 134), or alternatively, ask your fishmonger to do this for you. Cut slashes in a criss-cross pattern on one side of the mackerel.
2. Put the rosemary into the belly cavity of the fish and season lightly with salt and pepper and sprinkle with a little fresh lemon juice.
3. Heat the butter or oil in a large, heavy frying pan and brown the mackerel on each side for 3-4 minutes.
4. Add the remaining lemon juice and rind, then turn down the heat and continue to cook, just below simmering point, for a further 10 minutes or until the fish is tender.
5. Garnish with sprigs of rosemary and lemon slices and serve immediately with the pan juices poured over the mackerel.

HADDOCK IN A CURRY SAUCE

750 g (1½ lb) haddock fillets, skinned
1 onion, peeled and sliced
1 garlic clove, crushed
25 g (1 oz) butter
350 g (12 oz) long-grain rice, cooked, to serve
curry plant sprigs, to garnish (optional)

Marinade:
2 tablespoons lemon juice
1 teaspoon clear honey
salt
freshly ground black pepper
2 teaspoons curry powder
300 ml (½ pint) plain unsweetened yogurt
pinch of turmeric
1 teaspoon ground coriander seeds
2 teaspoons grated fresh root ginger
25 g (1 oz) butter (optional)

Preparation time: 20 minutes, plus chilling
Cooking time: about 40 minutes
Oven: 180°C, 350°F, Gas Mark 4

1. Combine all the marinade ingredients except the butter in a large glass or earthenware bowl. Cut the haddock into thick slices and put into the marinade. Cover and leave in a cool place for 1-2 hours to marinate.
2. Gently cook the onion and garlic in the butter, then place in the base of a lightly buttered baking dish.
3. Arrange the fish with its marinade over the onion, cover with a lid or foil, and bake in a preheated oven for 30 minutes or until the fish is tender.
4. Have ready a serving dish filled with the plain boiled rice, heaped up around the edge to make a rim, and lift the pieces of fish out of the dish and arrange in the centre of the rice.
5. Transfer the marinade to a small saucepan and heat gently, adding a few knobs of butter if you wish. Pour over the fish, and garnish with sprigs of curry plant, if using. Serve immediately with poppadoms.

ABOVE LEFT: Mackerel with lemon and rosemary
BELOW LEFT: Haddock in a curry sauce

HUSS WITH ALMONDS AND APPLE

450-750 g (1-1½ lb) huss fillets
150 ml (¼ pint) milk
2-3 tablespoons plain flour
pinch of salt
pinch of freshly ground black pepper
1 tablespoon oil
25 g (1 oz) butter
100 g (4 oz) blanched almonds, sliced
100 g (4 oz) dessert apple, cored and
    diced
2 tablespoons double cream
2 tablespoons plain unsweetened yogurt
pinch of freshly grated nutmeg
1 bunch spring onions, thinly sliced, to
    garnish

Preparation time: 20 minutes
Cooking time: about 10 minutes

Serve this dish with mangetout and boiled new potatoes tossed in butter and chopped parsley.

1. Cut the fish into bite-sized pieces. Then dip them first in the milk then lightly dust in flour which has been seasoned with salt and pepper.
2. Gently fry the fish in hot oil and butter in a heavy frying pan. Drain on paper towels and transfer to a heated serving plate.
3. Stir the almonds and diced apple into the pan juices and continue frying until lightly browned, then remove the pan from the heat and stir in the double cream and yogurt, scraping the bottom of the pan to incorporate all the cooking juices.
4. Add the nutmeg and stir until well blended. Pour over the fish and serve immediately with a garnish of finely sliced spring onions.

SMOKED MACKEREL WITH STIR-FRIED VEGETABLES

2 tablespoons sunflower oil
6 medium carrots, scraped and thinly sliced
225 g (8 oz) broccoli, trimmed and cut into
    florets
75 g (3 oz) mushrooms, wiped and thickly
    sliced
4 boiled potatoes, diced
2 tomatoes, skinned and quartered
4 smoked mackerel fillets, roughly flaked
½ melon, flesh chopped into bite-sized
    pieces
salt
freshly ground black pepper

To garnish:
lemon slices
fennel sprigs

Preparation time: 15 minutes
Cooking time: about 5 minutes

The combination of the smoked fish with crunchy stir-fried vegetables is quite delightful.

1. Heat the oil in a wok or large, heavy, shallow frying pan. Add the carrots, then the broccoli florets, stir-fry for 30 seconds, then add the mushrooms, potatoes, tomatoes and mackerel.
2. Continue stir-frying for 1 minute, add the melon and stir in briskly until just heated through.
3. Season to taste with salt and pepper, garnish with lemon slices and sprigs of fennel and serve immediately.

ABOVE RIGHT: Huss with almonds and apple
BELOW RIGHT: Smoked mackerel with stir-fried vegetables

STUFFED GREY MULLET

SERVES 2-4

2 grey mullet, about 750 g (1½ lb) in
  weight
75 g (3 oz) fresh breadcrumbs
1 tablespoon chopped parsley
2 tablespoons finely chopped onion
3 bay leaves, crumbled
grated rind of 1 lemon
salt
freshly ground black pepper
1 egg, beaten
1 webb's lettuce
450 g (1 lb) potatoes
150 ml (¼ pint) dry cider
1 lemon, sliced
a little butter
1 tablespoon crème fraîche or plain
  unsweetened yogurt

Preparation time: 35 minutes
Cooking time: about 40 minutes
Oven: 180°C, 350°F, Gas Mark 3

Grey mullet is one of my favourite fish – but does not seem to be generally well-known and recipes for this handsome fish are hard to come by. This recipe uses ordinary ingredients in a creative way – the resulting dish looks as though you have spent hours in the kitchen, and yet the preparation is very simple and easy. Use the heart of the lettuce to make a green salad.

1. Scale, clean and bone the mullet (see pages 134 and 135), or alternatively ask your fishmonger to do this for you. Wash and pat the fish dry with paper towels.
2. Combine the breadcrumbs, chopped parsley, onion, crumbled bay leaves, juice and grated rind of the lemon, salt and pepper and bind with the beaten egg to make a firm, moist stuffing. Stuff the mullet and set aside.
3. Blanch the large green outer leaves of the lettuce in a pan of boiling salted water for 1-2 minutes, drain and pat dry with

paper towels.
4. Arrange slices of lemon along the mullet, and dot with little knobs of butter. Wrap up the mullet with the lettuce leaves and place in a baking dish.
5. Peel and dice the potatoes and pack around the mullet, season with salt and pepper and pour over the cider.
6. Bake in a preheated oven for 35-40 minutes.
7. Carefully lift out the mullet and put on a heated serving dish – use a slotted spoon to take the potatoes out and surround the mullet with them.
8. Pour the cooking juices into a saucepan and boil to reduce, lower the heat and swirl in the crème fraîche or yogurt.
9. Peel back the lettuce leaves and pour over the sauce.
10. The fish will slice into beautiful cutlets.

FISH PIE

450 g (1 lb) potatoes, scrubbed
50 g (2 oz) butter
450 g (1 lb) smoked haddock fillets,
  skinned and flaked
100 g (4 oz) mushrooms, wiped and sliced
1×225 g (8 oz) can chopped tomatoes
150 ml (¼ pint) soured cream
50 g (2 oz) Cheddar cheese, grated

Preparation time: 35 minutes
Cooking time: 40-45 minutes
Oven: 180°C, 350°F, Gas Mark 4

ABOVE LEFT: Stuffed grey mullet
BELOW LEFT: Fish pie

This is a very simple pie. I like to use smoked haddock for this but you could use a mixture of firm white fish such as cod or coley and mix it with half the amount of smoked haddock.

1. Boil the potatoes for about 15 minutes until just tender.
2. Cool and cut them into thin slices.
3. Using a little of the butter, lightly grease a casserole or baking dish and arrange a layer of sliced potatoes on the base.
4. Put the haddock, mushrooms and tomatoes with their juice into a bowl, add the soured cream and combine well.
5. Tip this mixture on top of the potato layer, then arrange another layer of potato

on top. Dot with small knobs of butter and the grated cheese.
6. Bake the pie in a preheated oven for 25-30 minutes.

BAKED PLAICE WITH ORANGES

SERVES 4-6
50 g (2 oz) butter
900 g (2 lb) plaice fillets, folded over
grated rind and juice of 1 lemon
salt
freshly ground black pepper
cayenne
2 oranges, peeled and sliced

To garnish:
marjoram sprigs
orange twists
lemon twists

Preparation time: 25 minutes
Cooking time: 10-15 minutes
Oven: 200°C, 400°F, Gas Mark 6

1. Lightly butter an ovenproof dish and place the folded plaice fillets on the bottom.
2. Dot the fillets with the remaining butter and add the grated rind and juice of the lemon, making sure the surface of the fish is well coated.
3. Season with salt and pepper and sprinkle with cayenne.
4. Add the sliced oranges and bake in a preheated oven for 10-15 minutes.
5. Serve with the juices left from baking and garnish with sprigs of marjoram and orange and lemon twists.

SAVOURY STUFFED PLAICE FILLETS

4 plaice fillets, skinned and halved
  lengthways
3 tablespoons dry white wine
25 g (1 oz) butter
1-2 tablespoons plain unsweetened yogurt
grilled cherry tomatoes, to serve

Stuffing:
50 g (2 oz) fresh wholemeal breadcrumbs
2 tablespoons finely chopped gherkins
2 tablespoons finely chopped parsley
2 tablespoons finely chopped spring onions
salt
freshly ground black pepper
1 egg, beaten, to bind

To garnish:
coriander sprigs
spring onion tassels

Preparation time: 20 minutes
Cooking time: 20-25 minutes
Oven: 200°C, 400°F, Gas Mark 6

1. Combine the stuffing ingredients together thoroughly.
2. Place a spoonful of the stuffing on each halved plaice fillet and roll up from the head to the tail.
3. Arrange the stuffed, rolled plaice fillets on a buttered ovenproof dish, making sure the tail of each fillet is tucked neatly underneath the roll.
4. Add the wine, dot each fillet with a tiny knob of butter and bake in a preheated oven for 15-20 minutes.
5. Transfer the fillets to a warm serving dish. Pour the cooking juices in a saucepan and boil to reduce, lower the heat and add the yogurt, taste and adjust the seasoning if necessary, then pour the sauce over the fillets.
6. Serve the fish with grilled cherry tomatoes and garnish with sprigs of coriander and spring onion tassels.

ABOVE RIGHT: Baked plaice with oranges
BELOW RIGHT: Savoury stuffed plaice fillets

FISH COBBLER

SERVES 6

1 onion, peeled and chopped
1 garlic clove, crushed
1 tablespoon oil
25 g (1 oz) butter
2 carrots, scraped and thinly sliced
2 courgettes, sliced
2 celery sticks, trimmed and finely sliced
1×400 g (14 oz) can tomatoes or 750 g
  (1½ lb) ripe fresh tomatoes, skinned and
  roughly chopped
1 tablespoon chopped fresh green herbs or
  1 teaspoon dried parsley and thyme
1 bay leaf
about 150 ml (¼ pint) fish stock (see
  page 139) or white wine
salt
freshly ground black pepper
750 g (1½ lb) huss, coley or whiting fillets,
  skinned and cut into bite-sized pieces
75 g (3 oz) Parmesan or Cheddar cheese,
  grated

Scones:
100 g (4 oz) wholemeal flour
100 g (4 oz) plain flour
4 teaspoons baking powder
pinch of salt
50 g (2 oz) butter or margarine
1 tablespoon chopped fresh or 1 teaspoon
  dried parsley
1 tablespoon chopped fresh or 1 teaspoon
  dried thyme
¼ teaspoon paprika
a little milk

Preparation time: about 45 minutes
Cooking time: about 40 minutes
Oven: 220°C, 425°F, Gas Mark 7

To save time you can prepare this dish in advance, making the scone topping just before cooking.

1. In a heavy saucepan, soften the onion and garlic in the oil and butter over a gentle heat.
2. Add the carrots, courgettes and celery and continue to cook for about 10 minutes, stirring occasionally.
3. Add the tomatoes, herbs, stock or wine, bring up to simmering point and cook gently for about 6 minutes.
4. Season to taste with salt and pepper. Add the fish and cook for 2 minutes, taking care not to break up the fish as you gently stir around.
5. Transfer to a lightly buttered pie or baking dish.
6. To make the scone topping, sift together the flours, baking powder and salt then rub in the butter or margarine. Add the herbs and paprika.

7. Form into a light scone dough with the milk. Roll out on a floured board and cut out the scones with a cutter.
8. Arrange the scones in an overlapping ring around the edge of the dish and brush with a little milk.
9. Sprinkle the cheese over the scones and bake in a preheated oven for 15 minutes or until the scones have risen and browned.

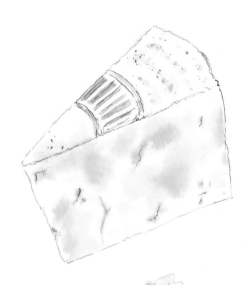

LEFT: Fish cobbler

PLAICE WITH SPICY MARINADE

4 medium plaice, cleaned

Marinade:
150 g (5 oz) plain unsweetened yogurt
2 tablespoons tomato purée
2 garlic cloves, crushed
2 tablespoons fresh lemon juice
1 onion, peeled and finely chopped
1-2 teaspoons chilli powder, to taste
1 teaspoon coriander seeds, crushed
½ teaspoon ground turmeric
salt
freshly ground black pepper

To garnish:
chervil sprigs
lime wedges

Preparation time: 25 minutes, plus chilling
Cooking time: about 10 minutes

If plaice is unavailable substitute with lemon sole, megrim, witch or dab.

1. Prepare and wash the fish, pat dry with paper towels and cut slashes in a criss-cross pattern on both sides.
2. Mix the marinade ingredients together to make a paste, either in a food processor or blender, or by hand.
3. Smother the fish all over with this marinade, making sure it penetrates all the slashes, and leave it in a cool place for about 2-3 hours.
4. Grill the fish under a moderate heat for about 5 minutes on each side, brushing the plaice with the remaining marinade occasionally.
5. Transfer to individual warmed plates or a serving dish and dribble the juices from the grill pan over the fish, finishing with a garnish of chervil sprigs and lime wedges.
6. Accompany with plain boiled potatoes with snipped chives, and a mixed pepper salad.

SCAMPI PROVENCAL

450 g (1 lb) peeled scampi (Dublin Bay prawns)
court bouillon (see page 139)
25 g (1 oz) butter
1 small onion, peeled and finely chopped
1 garlic clove, crushed
450 g (1 lb) tomatoes, peeled and chopped
1 tablespoon tomato purée
1 tablespoon chopped mixed herbs
2 tablespoons dry white wine (optional)
salt
freshly ground black pepper

Preparation time: 20 minutes
Cooking time: about 20 minutes

1. Poach the scampi in the court bouillon for 5-7 minutes, then drain and keep the scampi warm.
2. Melt the butter in a saucepan and add the onion and garlic. Soften for a few minutes before adding the chopped tomato, tomato purée, herbs, wine, if using, and season with salt and pepper to taste. Heat the sauce gently until bubbling.
3. For a smooth sauce, blend in a liquidiser or food processor, or push through a sieve.
4. Add the scampi to the sauce and heat through. Serve on a bed of parsleyed rice.

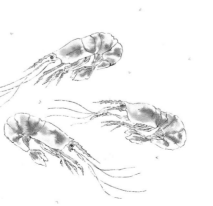

ABOVE RIGHT: Plaice with spicy marinade
BELOW RIGHT: Scampi provençal

SOLE A LA MEUNIERE

SERVES 3-4
6-8 large sole fillets
100 g (4 oz) plain flour
salt
freshly ground black pepper
150 ml (¼ pint) milk
175 g (6 oz) butter
2 tablespoons fresh lemon juice
2 tablespoons coarsely chopped fresh parsley
1 lemon, quartered, to garnish

Preparation time: 15 minutes
Cooking time: about 15 minutes

1. Rinse the fillets under cold running water and pat dry with paper towels.
2. Season the flour with salt and pepper. Dip the fillets in the milk, drain and coat lightly in the seasoned flour.
3. Melt 100 g (4 oz) of the butter in a heavy pan, taking care not to let it burn. Fry the fillets in the butter until golden brown on both sides. Place the fish fillets on a hot serving dish and keep warm.
4. Wipe out the pan with paper towels and melt the remaining butter in the pan, cook the butter until golden brown. Immediately add the lemon juice and parsley, taste and adjust the seasoning if necessary.

5. Pour the buttery sauce over the fish and garnish with lemon wedges.
6. Serve with grated potato fritters, young spinach leaves and sliced corn-on-the-cob.

SEAFOOD PANCAKES

SERVES 4-6
a little oil
225 g (8 oz) cooked white fish fillets,
 skinned and cut into bite-sized pieces
225 g (8 oz) peeled cooked prawns
1 quantity mornay sauce (see page 139)

Pancake batter:
100 g (4 oz) plain flour
pinch of salt
1 egg, beaten
300 ml (½ pint) milk
½ quantity watercress sauce (see page 141),
 to serve (optional)

To garnish:
lemon slices, halved
whole, cooked, unpeeled prawns
watercress sprigs

Preparation time: 30 minutes
Cooking time: about 20 minutes

ABOVE LEFT: Sole à la meuniere
BELOW LEFT: Seafood pancakes

1. First make the pancake batter, mix together the flour and salt, make a well in the centre and add the beaten egg and half the milk.
2. Gradually work in the flour and beat until smooth. Add the remaining milk a little at a time and stir well. Leave the batter to stand.
3. Heat a 15 cm (6 inch) frying pan and add a few drops of oil. Pour in 1 tablespoon of the batter and tilt the pan to coat the bottom evenly. Cook the pancake until the underside is brown, then carefully turn over and cook the other side for a further 10 seconds.
4. Turn the pancake onto a warmed plate. Repeat with the remaining batter making 12 pancakes in total. Stack, interleaved with greaseproof paper as they are cooked; keep warm.
5. Stir the fish pieces and prawns into the hot mornay sauce.
6. Make the pancakes into cones by folding them in half then in half again and fill with the sauce.

7. Garnish with halved lemon slices, whole prawns and sprigs of watercress. Serve with the watercress sauce, if using.

FISH, COURGETTE AND BROWN RICE BAKE

4-6 courgettes
450-750 g (1-1½ lb) white fish fillets
salt
freshly ground black pepper
4 tomatoes, peeled and sliced
1 onion, peeled and finely chopped
2 garlic cloves, crushed
2 tablespoons sunflower oil
450 g (1 lb) cooked brown rice
1 bunch parsley, chopped
4 tablespoons chopped herbs, as available
50 g (2 oz) Cheddar cheese, grated (optional)
tomato and courgette slices, to garnish

Sauce:
25 g (1 oz) unsalted butter
25 g (1 oz) plain flour
300 ml (½ pint) milk
salt
freshly ground black pepper
50 g (2 oz) cheese, grated
1 egg, beaten (optional)

Preparation time: 30 minutes
Cooking time: about 50 minutes
Oven: 200°C, 400°F, Gas Mark 6

This pie is really scrumptious. I like to let it settle for a few minutes before serving with hot, freshly cooked green vegetables.

1. Thinly slice the courgettes and arrange over the base and up the sides of a lightly buttered baking dish.
2. Slice the fillets into thick strips and pack into the dish – season with salt and pepper. Cover with the slices of tomato.
3. Soften the onion and garlic in the oil. Mix into the cooked brown rice and add all the herbs. Top the pie with this mixture.
4. Make the sauce. Melt the butter in a saucepan, add the flour and stir continuously for 2 minutes over a low heat. Remove the pan from the heat and gradually add the milk, stirring all the time. Season with salt and pepper, to taste. Return the pan to a low heat, bring to the boil and cook for 2-3 minutes, stirring constantly until the sauce thickens. Remove from the heat and stir in the cheese. Beat in the egg for a thicker consistency, if desired.
5. Pour the sauce over the top of the pie, sprinkle over the cheese, if using, and bake in a preheated oven for 30 minutes.
6. Garnish the pie with slices of tomato and courgette.

SOLE WITH GHERKIN SAUCE

SERVES 2
4 lemon sole fillets
salt
freshly ground black pepper
25 g (1 oz) butter
150 ml (¼ pint) soured cream
300 ml (½ pint) fish stock (see page 139)
2-3 gherkins, sliced

To garnish:
chervil sprigs
marjoram sprigs

Preparation time: 15 minutes
Cooking time: about 15 minutes

You can use plaice, witch, megrim or dab instead of the lemon sole in this recipe.

1. Season the sole fillets with salt and pepper to taste, and dot with the butter.
2. Grill the fish under a moderate heat for about 5 minutes each side (according to the thickness of the fillets) – be careful not to overcook.
3. Transfer to a warm serving dish, and keep hot.
4. Combine the soured cream and fish stock, and heat carefully to just under boiling point. Add the sliced gherkins and cook gently for 1 minute.

5. Pour the sauce over the fillets, garnish with sprigs of chervil and marjoram and serve immediately with ribbons of carrot and courgette or fresh bread and a simple crisp green salad.

ABOVE RIGHT: Fish, courgette and brown rice bake
BELOW RIGHT: Sole with gherkin sauce

MUSSELS WITH SPAGHETTI

1.2 litres (2 pints) fresh mussels
150 ml (¼ pint) dry red wine
2 tablespoons olive oil
1 onion, peeled and finely chopped
2 garlic cloves, crushed
½-1 teaspoon dried oregano
1×400 g (14 oz) can chopped tomatoes
50 g (2 oz) tomato purée
salt
freshly ground black pepper
400 g (14 oz) spaghetti
squeeze of fresh lemon juice, to serve

To garnish:
1 tablespoon chopped parsley
oregano sprigs

Preparation time: 25 minutes
Cooking time: 25-30 minutes

1. Prepare the mussels, scrub them well and remove the beards (see page 137). Discard any which are open and do not close when lightly tapped. Put the mussels in a large pan with the wine and steam them open. Cook for 5 minutes. Discard any that do not open during cooking.
2. Heat the olive oil and add the onion and garlic. Cook until softened. Add the oregano, tomatoes and tomato purée, and wine liquor from the mussels, and cook until the sauce is thick and reduced somewhat. Season to taste with salt and pepper.
3. Meanwhile, cook the spaghetti in lots of boiling salted water, into which you have added a drop of oil to prevent the spaghetti sticking. It will take about 12 minutes to cook and should be *al dente* (with a firm bite).

4. Drain the spaghetti through a colander and put into a large warmed serving dish and stir in the tomato sauce, and mussels in their shells.
5. Garnish with the chopped parsley and sprigs of oregano and squeeze over a little fresh lemon juice.

CRISPY FISH HOTPOT

SERVES 4-6
350 g (12 oz) courgettes, thinly sliced
2 red dessert apples, cored and thinly sliced
1 large onion, peeled and sliced
1 teaspoon dried sage
750 g (1½ lb) huss fillets, cut into small chunks
salt
freshly ground black pepper
1 teaspoon dried mustard powder
50 g (2 oz) fresh breadcrumbs
25 g (1 oz) butter
sage sprig, to garnish

Preparation time: 30 minutes
Cooking time: 55 minutes
Oven: 190°C, 375°F, Gas Mark 5

ABOVE LEFT: Mussels with spaghetti
BELOW LEFT: Crispy fish hotpot

This tasty fish hotpot goes well with chunky sautéed potatoes and steamed whole green beans.

1. Layer a greased ovenproof dish with the sliced courgettes, apples and onion. Sprinkle with the dried sage, cover with foil and bake in a preheated oven for 30 minutes.
2. Remove the dish from the oven and lift off the foil. Place the huss chunks on top of the layers of cooked courgettes, apples and onion, and season well with salt and pepper.
3. Mix together the mustard powder and the fresh breadcrumbs and sprinkle the mixture over the fish chunks. Dot with the butter and return to the oven for another 25 minutes.
4. Remove the hotpot from the oven, garnish with a sprig of sage and serve immediately.

To make fresh breadcrumbs use 1-2 day old white or wholemeal bread or a mixture of the two. The bread should not be too dry or it will not make fine crumbs, nor should it be very fresh, as it tends to cling together in a doughy ball.

Rub pieces of bread through a wire sieve or use a food processor or blender if you have one. To make breadcrumbs in a food processor use the metal chopping blade and drop cubes of bread into the bowl through the feed tube and process for 5-10 seconds. If using a blender drop a few cubes of bread at a time through the hole in the lid of the blender while the motor is running at high speed.

ENTERTAINING

Considering the wealth of seafood available it is surprising how infrequently we consider using it, especially when entertaining. Imagine a beautiful baked sea bass, so simple to cook and superb in taste. Think of the silvery skin of the herring, quickly baked and served with an elegant salad and pretty fruit sauce – what could be more appealing to the eye and delicious to eat.

Salmon with three sauces (see page 72)

SEA BASS WITH GINGER

1 medium sea bass, cleaned
pinch of salt
pinch of sugar
1 tablespoon sesame oil
1 tablespoon soy sauce
1 bunch spring onions
2 large garlic cloves
2×4 cm (1½ inch) pieces of fresh root
  ginger

To garnish:
spring onion tassels
lime slices
red and yellow pepper slices

Preparation time: 25 minutes
Cooking time: 20 minutes
Oven: 180°C, 350°F, Gas Mark 4

Sea bass is a beautiful, silvery fish – rather similar in shape to salmon but more bony. This recipe is typically Chinese in its use of ingredients – especially the combination of fresh root ginger and spring onions.

1. Rub the sea bass with the salt, sugar, sesame oil and soy sauce.
2. Chop the spring onions, garlic and ginger, and put half of these ingredients in a layer on the bottom of a lightly greased sheet of foil. Place the sea bass on top, and cover with the remaining mixture.

3. Wrap the foil up loosely, and bake in a preheated oven for 20 minutes or until the fish is tender. Serve in its own cooking juices with a garnish of spring onion tassels, slices of lime and slices of red and yellow pepper.

BRILL WITH LEMON SAUCE

4 brill fillets
100 g (4 oz) mushrooms
50 g (2 oz) butter
salt
freshly ground black pepper
2 tablespoons fresh lemon juice
4 tablespoons white wine

Sauce:
2 tablespoons fresh lemon juice
2 tablespoons chopped parsley
300 ml (½ pint) fish stock (see page 139)
1 tablespoon plain flour
2 eggs

To garnish:
lemon twists
parsley sprigs

Preparation time: 25 minutes
Cooking time: about 30 minutes
Oven: 180°C, 350°F, Gas Mark 4

1. Wash the brill fillets and pat dry with paper towels; skin the fillets or alternatively leave them as they are.
2. Cut the mushrooms into thin slices. Lightly butter an ovenproof dish and arrange the mushrooms on the base.
3. Fold the brill fillets in half and lay them on top of the mushrooms. Season with salt and pepper, and pour the lemon juice over them.
4. Add enough wine to moisten the mushrooms and dot the top of the fillets with a few knobs of the butter.
5. Bake in a preheated oven for 20 minutes, until the fillets are tender.
6. Put all the sauce ingredients into the bowl of a food processor or blender and process until smooth. Pour into the top of a double boiler, or alternatively pour into a heatproof bowl and set over a saucepan of simmering water: do not let the bowl touch the water.
7. Whisk the sauce constantly over a low heat until it thickens, then season with salt and pepper and add a little of the cooking juices from the brill dish.
8. Arrange the folded fillets of brill carefully on a warmed serving dish, pour over some of the sauce and sprinkle the mushrooms over the top. Garnish with lemon twists and parsley sprigs. Serve the remaining sauce separately.

ABOVE RIGHT: Sea bass with ginger
BELOW RIGHT: Brill with lemon sauce

JOHN DORY WITH WINE

SERVES 2
1 medium John Dory
50 g (2 oz) butter
150 ml (¼ pint) dry white wine
2 tablespoons quark or low-fat curd cheese
salt
freshly ground black pepper
coriander sprigs, to garnish

Preparation time: 10 minutes
Cooking time: about 20 minutes

1. Prepare the fish by removing the 4 fillets (see page 136). Leave the skin on the fillets to help keep them in shape.
2. Heat the butter in a heavy frying pan and fry the fillets gently on both sides for 2 minutes. Turn down the heat, add the wine and cook gently for another 10 minutes.
3. Transfer the fish to a warm serving dish.
4. Reduce the fish cooking liquor, cool slightly, then stir in the quark or low-fat curd cheese and season to taste with salt and pepper.
5. Pour the sauce over the fillets, garnish with sprigs of coriander and serve immediately with tiny new potatoes tossed in butter and chopped parsley and a green vegetable.

MARINATED HERRING WITH BLACKBERRY SAUCE

4 medium herring
1 onion, peeled and roughly chopped
10 cloves
2 bay leaves
1 tablespoon chopped parsley
1 tablespoon chopped thyme
pinch of salt
crushed black peppercorns
3 tablespoons fresh lemon juice
300 ml (½ pint) white wine vinegar
300 ml (½ pint) water

Blackberry sauce:
2 dessert apples
225 g (8 oz) blackberries
1 tablespoon sugar
3 tablespoons red wine
½ teaspoon ground cinnamon
2 cloves
2 tablespoons plain unsweetened yogurt

Preparation time: 25 minutes
Cooking time: 30-35 minutes
Oven: 180°C, 350°F, Gas Mark 4

ABOVE LEFT: John Dory with wine
BELOW LEFT: Marinated herring with blackberry sauce

This tasty dish can be served warm or chilled. A green salad makes a good accompaniment.

1. Clean, split and bone the herring (see pages 134 and 135), and roll up from head to tail. Place in a large baking dish, sprinkle with the onion, cloves, bay leaves, parsley, thyme, salt, peppercorns and lemon juice then pour over the wine vinegar and water.

2. Bake the herring in a preheated oven for 20-25 minutes.
3. Using a slotted spoon, lift out the fish and arrange on a serving dish. Reserve 2 tablespoons of the cooking liquor. Keep warm if you wish to serve hot or alternatively leave to chill in the refrigerator.
4. Make the blackberry sauce. Peel, core and chop the apples. Place the blackberries, apple, sugar and a little water in a saucepan and bring to the boil. Then add the wine, spices and the reserved fish cooking liquor. Cook gently for about 5 minutes. Swirl in the yogurt and serve hot or chilled as required.

RED MULLET WITH ORANGE AND FENNEL

SERVES 2

2 large red mullet
2 bulbs fennel, trimmed, sliced and poached
  in a little water or 2 bunches wild fennel
2 oranges
salt
freshly ground black pepper
50 g (2 oz) butter
halved lime slices, to garnish

Preparation time: 20 minutes
Cooking time: 25 minutes
Oven: 200°C, 400°F, Gas Mark 6

This is my favourite way of baking either red or grey mullet whole. Wild fennel (its feathery leaves resemble those of the cultivated bulbs you can buy in the shops) is very common around the seaside and the bruised stalks of this plant give a lovely fragrant taste to all sorts of fish. Try serving this dish with spinach and parsleyed potatoes.

1. Clean the whole mullet (see page 134) or alternatively ask your fishmonger to do this for you.
2. Arrange a layer of half the poached fennel slices in the bottom of a greased ovenproof dish and put the mullet on top of this.
3. Peel the oranges and cut into thin slices, reserving any juice. Surround and cover the fish with the orange slices and add any reserved juice, season with salt and pepper and cover the fish with the remaining fennel.
4. Dot with butter and bake in a preheated oven for about 25 minutes, or until the fish is cooked. (If using wild fennel, bruise and slightly break a few twigs, place in the dish and put the mullet on top, then scatter with the chopped leaves.)
5. Serve immediately, with the cooked orange slices, juices from the dish and garnish with halved lime slices and any sprigs of the feathery fennel leaves.

MONKFISH AND VEGETABLE PARCELS WITH SAFFRON SAUCE

450 g (1 lb) monkfish
2 medium carrots, scraped and cut into
  matchsticks
2 celery sticks, trimmed and cut into
  matchsticks
1 medium onion, peeled and very finely
  sliced into half rings
1 red pepper, cored, seeded and cut into
  matchsticks
2 tablespoons fresh lemon juice
3 tablespoons white wine
salt
freshly ground black pepper
4 tablespoons hot saffron sauce (see
  page 140)

Preparation time: 35 minutes
Cooking time: about 10 minutes

By steaming these parcels the vegetables stay slightly crunchy and therefore make a lovely contrast to the tender flesh of the monkfish.

1. Cut out four large pieces of foil and lightly butter.
2. Skin and bone the monkfish (see pages 135 and 136) and cut into medallions. Arrange a few medallions of monkfish in the centre of each piece of foil and surround them with small bundles of the prepared vegetables.
3. Sprinkle with the lemon juice and the white wine and season lightly with salt and pepper.
4. Bring the corners of the foil together and crimp the edges so that the parcels are totally sealed.
5. Place the parcels in a steamer or between 2 plates over a pan of boiling water, and steam for about 10 minutes or until the fish is tender.
6. Once the fish is cooked open the parcels and put 1 tablespoon of the saffron sauce on the fish – the juices and sauce mingle and taste delicious. Serve immediately.

ABOVE RIGHT: Red mullet with orange and fennel
BELOW RIGHT: Monkfish and vegetable parcels with saffron sauce

PLAICE STUFFED WITH SHRIMPS AND SCALLOPS

8 medium prepared scallops
50 g (2 oz) butter
150 ml (¼ pint) dry white wine
4 medium boned plaice
150 ml (¼ pint) hot béchamel sauce (see
 page 139)
100 g (4 oz) peeled cooked prawns
salt
freshly ground black pepper
squeeze of fresh lemon juice

To garnish:
parsley sprigs
whole, cooked unpeeled prawns
lemon wedges

Preparation time: 25 minutes
Cooking time: about 25 minutes
Oven: 180°C, 350°F, Gas Mark 4

1. Remove the coral from the scallops and slice the white flesh.
2. Sauté the white flesh gently, with the corals, in the butter for 2 minutes, then add the wine and continue to cook for a further 3-4 minutes.
3. Remove the scallops with a slotted spoon and keep warm on a heated plate. Reserve any stock.
4. Stir 3-4 tablespoons of stock from the scallops into the béchamel sauce and mix in the prawns and white scallop flesh. Season with salt and pepper to taste.
5. Stuff the scallop and prawn mixture into the cavities of the plaice, arrange the plaice on a lightly buttered baking dish, squeeze a little lemon juice all over and dot with butter.
6. Bake in a preheated oven for about

20 minutes, until tender.
7. When the fish is cooked, serve on 4 individual warmed plates and garnish with the scallop corals, sprigs of parsley, cooked unpeeled prawns and lemon wedges.

HALIBUT IN VERMOUTH

1 onion, peeled and finely chopped
1 garlic clove, crushed
50 g (2 oz) butter
750 g (1½ lb) halibut, skinned and cut into
 bite-sized pieces
about 150 ml (¼ pint) dry vermouth
2 tablespoons fromage blanc or single cream
1 tablespoon chopped parsley
salt
freshly ground black pepper
dill sprigs, to garnish

Preparation time: 20 minutes
Cooking time: about 15 minutes

1. Soften the onion and garlic in the butter then add the halibut. Continue cooking for 2-3 minutes before adding sufficient vermouth to cover the fish.
2. Poach the halibut in the vermouth for about 5 minutes, then remove the halibut from the pan and keep warm.

3. Boil the cooking liquor to reduce by half and add the fromage blanc or cream and the parsley.
4. Season to taste with salt and pepper and use the liquor to moisten the halibut.
5. Garnish with sprigs of dill and serve with mangetout and carrot sticks.

ABOVE LEFT: Plaice stuffed with shrimps
and scallops
BELOW LEFT: Halibut in vermouth

SALMON WITH THREE SAUCES

SERVES 8-10
1 salmon, about 2 kg (4½ lb) in weight,
  cleaned
salt
freshly ground black pepper
50 g (2 oz) butter, melted
lettuce leaves, to serve

Avocado sauce:
1 ripe avocado
150 ml (¼ pint) plain unsweetened yogurt
2-4 tablespoons fresh lemon juice

Horseradish sauce:
1-2 tablespoons grated horseradish
150 ml (¼ pint) soured cream
50 g (2 oz) walnuts, chopped

Cocktail sauce:
1-2 tablespoons tomato ketchup
150 ml (¼ pint) mayonnaise (see page 140)
a few drops of Tabasco sauce

To garnish:
cucumber slices
lemon slices
dill sprigs
chervil sprigs

Preparation time: about 1 hour, plus chilling
Cooking time: about 1 hour
Oven: 150°C, 300°F, Gas Mark 2

You can choose just 1 of the sauces to serve with the salmon, but all the 3 together are particularly attractive.

1. Wash the salmon belly cavity, then pat dry with paper towels and season lightly with salt and pepper.
2. Grease a large sheet of foil with the melted butter. Place the salmon on to the foil, wrap up and put in a baking dish or tray and place in a preheated oven and bake for about 1 hour.
3. Remove the salmon from the oven and leave to cool.
4. Meanwhile, prepare the sauces. For the avocado sauce, peel and stone the avocado, place in a food processor or blender and add the yogurt, a little salt and pepper, and lemon juice to taste. Blend the sauce until smooth.
5. For the horseradish sauce, mix the grated horseradish with the soured cream, add salt and pepper to taste, then mix in the walnuts.
6. For the cocktail sauce, mix the tomato ketchup with the mayonnaise and add Tabasco to taste.

7. Chill the sauces until ready to serve.
8. Remove the salmon carefully from the foil and lay it on a clean working surface or large chopping board. Using a long, thin-bladed sharp knife, cut through the skin along the length of the backbone, across the tail and around the head. Using the blade of the knife, peel off the skin and pull off the fins. With the back of the knife, scrape away the shallow layer of brown-coloured flesh over the centre of the fish. Turn the salmon over and repeat.
9. Then cut down along the backbone of the fish, turn the knife flat and ease the fillet gently from the bone, and lift off. (This will have to be done in 2 pieces if it is a large fish.) At the head and tail, cut through the bone with kitchen scissors and peel away. Replace the upper fillet.
10. Gently lift the salmon on to individual plates, pour pools of the 3 sauces next to the salmon. Garnish with thinly sliced cucumber, lemon and sprigs of dill and chervil. Keep cool until ready to serve.

RIGHT: Salmon with three sauces

SOLE VERONIQUE

8 sole fillets, skinned and rolled
1 onion, peeled and sliced
1 bay leaf
sprig of parsley
150 ml (¼ pint) fish stock (see page 139)
pinch of salt
pinch of freshly ground black pepper
150-300 ml (¼-½ pint) dry white wine

Sauce:
25 g (1 oz) butter
25 g (1 oz) plain flour
150 ml (¼ pint) milk
salt
freshly ground black pepper
150 ml (¼ pint) double cream

To garnish:
about 20 seedless black grapes, halved
fennel sprigs

Preparation time: 25 minutes
Cooking time: about 40 minutes
Oven: 160°C, 325°F, Gas Mark 3

1. Place the sole fillets in a lightly buttered, ovenproof dish. Surround them with the onion, bay leaf, parsley, fish stock and a pinch each of salt and pepper.
2. Pour in the wine just to cover, and bake in a preheated oven for up to 20 minutes, according to the thickness of the fillets.
3. When cooked, transfer the fillets to a warmed serving dish and keep warm. Boil the strained cooking liquid and reduce it to 6 tablespoons.
4. Melt the butter in a saucepan, add the flour and stir for 2 minutes over a low heat. Remove from the heat and gradually stir in the milk and reduced stock and season with salt and pepper. Return the pan to a low heat, bring to the boil and cook for 2-3 minutes, stirring constantly until the sauce thickens. Remove from the heat and stir in the double cream.
5. Coat the sole fillets with this sauce, and garnish with the halved grapes and sprigs of fennel.
6. Serve immediately with tiny new potatoes tossed in butter and parsley.

LEFT: Sole Véronique

Sole is a lean, flat, oval seafish with firm white flesh. It has a delicate flavour and is easily digested. The freshness of sole is indicated by very white flesh, coloured gills and a sticky skin.

Dover sole is probably the best known and tastiest member of the sole family and the skin is brown or grey in colour.

Lemon sole, though in fact not a member of the same family as Dover sole, has a lovely delicate flavour and is less expensive than Dover sole.

Either whole or halved, seedless black or white grapes are suitable for Sole Véronique, a mixture of the two can also be used with stunning results. If seedless grapes are unavailable use grapes with seeds and simply half and deseed them.

SOLE BONNE FEMME

SERVES 4-6

4 shallots, peeled and chopped
100 g (4 oz) mushrooms, wiped and sliced
75 g (3 oz) butter
2 tablespoons parsley, chopped
1 kg (2 lb) sole fillets, halved lengthways
  and skinned
salt
freshly ground black pepper
4 tablespoons dry white wine
150 ml (¼ pint) fish stock (see page 139)
2 tablespoons lemon juice
25 g (1 oz) plain flour

To garnish:
parsley sprigs
lemon twists

Preparation time: 20 minutes
Cooking time: about 30 minutes
Oven: 180°C, 350°F, Gas Mark 4

1. Shallow fry the shallots and mushrooms in 50 g (2 oz) of the butter. Add the parsley then spread the mixture on the base of an ovenproof dish.

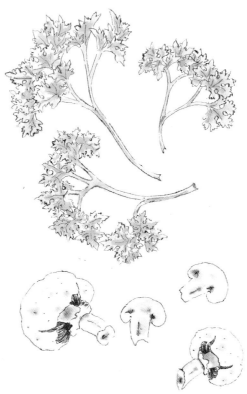

2. Roll up the sole fillets from head to tail, put into the dish and season well with salt and pepper.
3. Pour over the white wine, stock and lemon juice. Bake in a preheated oven for 15 minutes.
4. Transfer the sole to a heated serving dish. Fork together the remaining 25 g (1 oz) of butter with the 25 g (1 oz) of flour to form a paste – beurre manie – and use this to thicken the cooking liquid with the mushrooms. Add in small knobs to the boiling mushroom mixture, whisk until the butter melts and the sauce thickens.
5. Pour the sauce over the sole and serve hot, garnished with parsley and lemon.

RIGHT: Sole bonne femme

PAELLA

SERVES 8

1.75 litres (3 pints) mussels
1 medium cooked lobster or 225 g (8 oz)
  monkfish
350 g (12 oz) prepared squid
12 prepared scallops
1 red pepper, cored and seeded
1 green pepper, cored and seeded
6 tablespoons olive oil
2 large Spanish onions, peeled and finely
  chopped
1 kg (2 lb) long-grain rice
150 ml (¼ pint) dry white wine
1 litre (1¾ pints) fish stock (see page 139)
2-3 teaspoons saffron powder
2 bay leaves
225 g (8 oz) frozen petit pois
450 g (1 lb) peeled cooked prawns
salt
freshly ground black pepper

Preparation time: 35 minutes
Cooking time: about 25 minutes

Although there are endless variations of this dish, I have omitted one ingredient that should always be included in a classic paella – MEAT! I personally prefer the unadulterated taste of shellfish and fish. Traditionally this Spanish dish is eaten with a spoon.

1. Prepare the mussels, scrub well and remove the beards. Cook in a little water in a large pan until they have opened. Discard any that have not opened. Reserve the cooking liquor.
2. Shell the lobster (see page 138) or skin and bone the monkfish (see pages 135 and 136) and cut up the flesh.
3. Slice the squid into thin rings and slice the scallops.
4. Slice the red and green peppers into thin strips and gently cook in 2 tablespoons of the olive oil. Remove from the pan and keep warm.
5. Add the sliced squid and scallops (and monkfish if used) to the pan and turn them gently as they cook, then remove and keep warm. In a large paella dish or shallow pan, gently cook the onion in the remaining olive oil until transparent. Add the rice and fry gently for a few more minutes, then pour in the wine, fish stock and reserved mussel liquor. Bring up to simmering point, add the saffron powder and give a few careful stirs; then add the bay leaves.
6. After about 10-15 minutes the rice, now a lovely saffron yellow, should have absorbed the stock and you can stir in the petit pois.
7. Add the prawns, all the reserved fish and shellfish and the red and green pepper, and, again, give a few gentle stirs.
8. Let it heat through, taste and season with salt and pepper.
9. Remove the bay leaves and serve.

LEFT: Paella

SKATE IN ORANGE AND CIDER SAUCE

4 skate wings
1 small onion, peeled and finely chopped
300 ml (½ pint) dry cider
juice and rind of 1 orange
salt
freshly ground black pepper
capers
squeeze of fresh lemon juice
4 tablespoons double cream or fromage
  blanc
orange slices, peeled and quartered, to
  garnish

Preparation time: 15 minutes
Cooking time: about 30 minutes

1. Place the skate wings in a large shallow pan. Add the onion, cider, orange juice and pieces of thinly pared orange rind, then a pinch of salt and pepper. Bring slowly up to barely simmering point and poach for about 15 minutes.
2. Lift out the skate wings with a slotted spoon and place them on a warmed serving dish. Keep the skate warm.
3. Turn up the heat, add the capers and boil the cooking liquor until it is reduced and thick, then taste and adjust the seasoning if necessary. Add a squeeze of lemon juice, remove from the heat and swirl in the cream or fromage blanc.
4. Pour the sauce over the skate wings and serve immediately, garnished with quartered orange slices. Serve with a selection of green vegetables.

SKATE WITH BLACK BUTTER

750 g (1½ lb) skate wings, cut into wedges
600 ml (1 pint) court bouillon (see page
  139) or white wine and water
about 100 g (4 oz) butter
4 tablespoons lemon juice or white wine
  vinegar
1 tablespoon chopped parsley
1-2 tablespoons capers
lemon twists, to garnish

Preparation time: 10 minutes
Cooking time: about 20 minutes

The butter is not black at all in this dish, just melted over a medium heat until it turns a sizzling deep golden colour. Have all the ingredients ready as the success of this dish depends on cooking it quickly and serving immediately. Plain boiled potatoes are good with this dish to soak up the delicious juices and butter.

1. Poach the skate wings in the court bouillon or wine and water mixture for 15-20 minutes or until just tender, making sure that the liquid does not boil. Test with a fork: the flesh should flake easily.
2. Transfer the skate to a warm serving dish and keep warm.
3. Melt the butter in a pan until it turns a sizzling deep golden colour and pour it over the fish.
4. Put the lemon juice or white wine vinegar into the pan and stir furiously for about 20 seconds and pour this over the

fish as well, then scatter over the chopped parsley and capers.
5. Garnish with lemon twists and serve with vegetables of your choice.

ABOVE RIGHT: Skate in orange and cider sauce
BELOW RIGHT: Skate with black butter

TROUT WITH ALMONDS

plain flour, for coating
salt
freshly ground black pepper
4 medium trout, cleaned
100 g (4 oz) butter
100 g (4 oz) flaked almonds
2 tablespoons lemon juice

To garnish:
fennel sprigs
lemon wedges

Preparation time: 15 minutes
Cooking time: about 20 minutes

This classic dish combines the succulent texture of trout with the crisp crunchiness of buttery fried flaked almonds.

1. Season the flour with salt and pepper and dust over the trout.
2. Fry the trout in half the butter for 3-4 minutes on each side.
3. Remove the trout from the frying pan and keep warm.
4. Add the rest of the butter to the frying pan with the flaked almonds and fry gently until the almonds have turned a golden colour.
5. Add the lemon juice to the pan and season to taste with salt and pepper, then heat through thoroughly before pouring over the trout.
6. Garnish with sprigs of fennel and lemon wedges.

TROUT BAKED IN RED WINE

1 large onion, peeled and thinly sliced
1 large carrot, scraped and thinly sliced
2 tablespoons chopped parsley
1 bay leaf
4 trout, cleaned
salt
freshly ground black pepper
300 ml (½ pint) red wine
1 teaspoon anchovy sauce
50 g (2 oz) butter (optional)

To garnish:
1 tablespoon chopped parsley
bay leaves

Preparation time: 25 minutes
Cooking time: about 35 minutes
Oven: 190°C, 375°F, Gas Mark 5

1. Put a layer of the vegetables and herbs in a buttered ovenproof dish and place the trout on top, season well with salt and pepper and top with another layer of vegetables and herbs.
2. Pour over the wine and bake, covered with a lid or foil, in a preheated oven for 20-25 minutes.
3. Remove the trout from the dish and keep warm. Boil the juices and vegetables until well reduced. Add the anchovy sauce and butter, if using, and strain over the fish.
4. Garnish the trout with chopped parsley and bay leaves and serve with stir-fried vegetables.

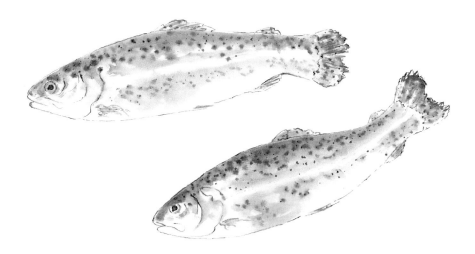

ABOVE LEFT: Trout with almonds
BELOW LEFT: Trout baked in red wine

LOBSTER THERMIDOR

*2 cooked lobsters, weighing about 750 g
  (1½ lb) each*
75 g (3 oz) butter
1 shallot, peeled and finely chopped
50 g (2 oz) plain flour
4 tablespoons dry white wine
300 ml (½ pint) fish stock (see page 139)
1 teaspoon prepared English mustard
salt
freshly ground black pepper
2 tablespoons fresh lemon juice (optional)
*4 tablespoons wholemeal breadcrumbs,
  browned in a little butter*
1 tablespoon chopped parsley

To garnish:
lime twists
lemon geranium sprigs (optional)

Preparation time: 30 minutes
Cooking time: 20 minutes

A gourmet dish for special occasions.

1. Open out the lobsters back-side down and, with a strong sharp knife, cut in half lengthways, taking care not to damage the shells. Alternatively, ask your fishmonger to do this for you.
2. Extract the meat from the body and claws (see page 138). Reserve the lobster shells and oil lightly.
3. Chop up the lobster flesh, and gently sauté in 25 g (1 oz) of the butter for 4 minutes, turning all the time, then remove from the pan and keep warm.
4. Melt the remaining butter in a saucepan and gently cook the shallot, then add the flour and cook for 1-2 minutes.
5. Remove from the heat and gradually stir in the wine and the fish stock. Return to a low heat and bring to the boil, stirring constantly until thickened. Cook for

2-3 minutes. Add the mustard, salt and pepper to taste, and a little fresh lemon juice, if desired.
6. Fold the lobster flesh into this sauce, and pour the mixture into the lightly oiled lobster shells.
7. Sprinkle the browned breadcrumbs over the mixture in the shells, and brown under a hot grill until golden and bubbling. Sprinkle with the chopped parsley, garnish with lime twists and lemon geranium sprigs, if using, and serve immediately with really fresh bread and a crisp green salad.

WHITING IN TOMATO AND BASIL SAUCE

salt
freshly ground black pepper
4 whiting fillets, halved and folded over
12 bruised leaves of basil
3-4 tablespoons dry white wine
basil sprigs and chives, to garnish

Sauce:
1 tablespoon olive oil
25 g (1 oz) butter
1 small onion, peeled and finely chopped
1 carrot, scraped and grated
6 ripe tomatoes, peeled, seeded and chopped
2 teaspoons tomato purée
2 tablespoons fresh chopped basil
2 tablespoons fromage blanc or soured cream
squeeze of fresh lemon juice

Preparation time: 30 minutes
Cooking time: about 30 minutes

1. Season the fillets with salt and pepper, place on a large piece of foil and cover with the bruised leaves of basil and the wine. Wrap up the foil to seal.
2. Set the foil parcel in a steamer and cook for about 10 minutes.
3. When cooked, transfer the fish to a warmed serving dish, keep warm and reserve the juices.
4. Whilst the fish is cooking, heat up the olive oil and butter in a heavy saucepan, soften the onion and carrot for 5 minutes, stirring and not allowing it to brown.
5. Add the tomatoes, tomato purée, basil and the reserved cooking juices from the fish and cook the sauce over a very low heat until cooked through.
6. Put this sauce into a food processor or blender and purée until smooth, return to the pan and reheat.

7. Add the fromage blanc or soured cream, season with salt and pepper, and add lemon juice to give a sharper taste.
8. Arrange the sauce and fillets on a warmed serving dish, garnish with sprigs of basil and chives and serve.

ABOVE RIGHT: Lobster thermidor
BELOW RIGHT: Whiting in tomato and basil sauce

SUPPERS AND SNACKS

There cannot be a more natural food which can be cooked as quickly and simply as fish. Busy families, and children in particular should be encouraged to eat more fish, try Fish and Sorrel Omelette and Smoked Haddock and Leek Flan for variations on a familiar theme. This chapter will fire your imagination and inspire you to think about fish on those occasions when a delicious, quick and nourishing meal is called for.

Seafood pilau (see page 95)

FETTUCCINE ALLA TROTA

1 tablespoon olive oil
1 medium onion, peeled and finely chopped
2 garlic cloves, finely chopped
4 smoked trout, boned and flaked
450 g (1 lb) fresh or dried fettuccine
pinch of salt
pinch of freshly ground black pepper
pinch of ground mace
300 ml (½ pint) whipping cream

To garnish:
1 tablespoon chopped parsley
1 teaspoon red lumpfish roe

Preparation time: 15 minutes
Cooking time: 2-15 minutes

This is a substantial and quickly made supper dish using smoked trout.

1. Heat the oil in a pan and add the onion and garlic and cook until softened, then add the flaked trout flesh.
2. Cook the fettuccine in plenty of boiling salted water until *al dente* – about 2-3 minutes for fresh pasta and 12 minutes for dried pasta.
3. Drain and add to the trout mixture, season to taste with the salt, pepper and mace then pour on the cream.
4. Toss together over a high heat for 1 minute and serve sprinkled with chopped parsley and red lumpfish roe.

SIZZLY WHITING WITH TANGY SAUCE

4 whiting fillets
50 g (2 oz) butter
1 tablespoon prepared English mustard
3 tablespoons single cream or plain
  unsweetened yogurt
2 teaspoons lemon juice
½ teaspoon Worcestershire sauce
1 tablespoon snipped chives
lemon slices, quartered, to garnish

Preparation time: 10 minutes
Cooking time: 15 minutes

1. Fry the whiting fillets in the butter for about 4 minutes each side, or alternatively cook under the grill, then place the fillets on a warmed serving dish.
2. Mix together the mustard, cream or yogurt, lemon juice and Worcestershire sauce and pour this into the pan. Heat through, stirring continuously, but do not boil.
3. Pour the sauce over the fish and sprinkle with snipped chives. Garnish with quartered lemon slices and serve hot with a selection of vegetables.

ABOVE RIGHT: Fettuccine alla trota
BELOW RIGHT: Sizzly whiting with tangy sauce

PAN-FRIED PIZZA

SERVES 4-6

Pizza dough:

225 g (8 oz) wholemeal or white plain
  flour, or half of each
pinch of salt
1 teaspoon baking powder
25-50 g (1-2 oz) butter
about 150 ml (¼ pint) milk

Topping:

1 medium onion, peeled and finely chopped
1 clove garlic, crushed
a little oil, for frying
1×400 g (14 oz) can chopped tomatoes
1 tablespoon chopped fresh or 1 teaspoon
  dried mixed herbs
225-350 g (8-12 oz) smoked mackerel,
  roughly flaked
100 g (4 oz) peeled cooked prawns
175 g (6 oz) Gruyère or Cheddar cheese
50 g (2 oz) black olives
sage sprigs, to garnish (optional)

Preparation time: 35 minutes
Cooking time: about 25 minutes

This scone-based pizza is very easy to make and cook. You could also make 4 individual pizzas, about 10 cm (4 inches) in diameter, and bake these on a lightly greased baking tray in an oven for about 10 minutes. Another good idea would be to use lightly buttered Yorkshire pudding tins for the bases. This is good with a homemade coleslaw.

1. Sift the flour, salt and baking powder together into a bowl, rub in the butter until the mixture resembles fine breadcrumbs, then add enough milk to form into a firm scone dough.

2. With cool fingers, lightly pat it into a round pizza shape on a floured work surface. It should be able to fit in a deep-sided frying pan.

3. Heat a little oil in the frying pan and put in the pizza base. Leave to fry gently for about 10 minutes, occasionally slipping a spatula around the edge of the pizza to prevent it sticking.

4. Meanwhile, soften the onion and garlic in a little hot oil. Add the tomatoes and herbs and continue to cook until the juice is reduced and the sauce is thick.

5. Spoon the tomato mixture on to the cooked pizza base and scatter over the flaked fish and prawns.

6. Either top the fish with grated cheese and olives or cut the cheese into strips and make a lattice pattern, arranging the olives in the little squares. Put the pizza under a hot grill and continue to cook until the topping is brown and bubbling.

7. Garnish with sprigs of sage, if using.

LEFT: Pan-fried pizza

Make a crunchy coleslaw to serve with this pizza using 1 medium white cabbage, cored and finely shredded, 4 medium carrots, coarsely grated, 1 small onion, finely sliced and 50 g (2 oz) seedless raisins. Mix all the ingredients together in a large bowl then add 8 tablespoons mayonnaise (see page 140) and season with salt and freshly ground black pepper. Toss the ingredients gently to coat with mayonnaise and to mix.

FISH AND SORREL OMELETTE

SERVES 2

6 eggs

4 tablespoons plain unsweetened yogurt

1 tablespoon chopped parsley

freshly ground black pepper

25 g (1 oz) butter

1 small onion or shallot, peeled and finely
    chopped

12 leaves of sorrel, or spinach, finely
    chopped

175 g (6 oz) cooked white fish fillets (such
    as cod, coley or haddock)

75 g (3 oz) cooked smoked fish fillets (such
    as kipper or mackerel)

Preparation time: 15 minutes
Cooking time: about 15 minutes

This provides a very good light lunch dish.
Try it with a crunchy red and green
pepper salad dressed with oil and vinegar
– a good contrast in texture!

1. Beat the eggs and yogurt together then
add the chopped parsley and season with
pepper to taste.
2. Melt the butter in a large omelette pan
and cook the onion until pale and soft.
Add the chopped sorrel or spinach and stir
for about 1 minute, until the leaves soften.

3. Add the fish, skinned and chopped into
chunks. Pour in the beaten egg mixture
and cook until the omelette is set. Finish
by browning under the grill.
4. Slide the unfolded omelette on to
a warmed serving plate and serve
immediately.

CHEESEY FISH BURGERS

350 g (12 oz) cooked, flaked white fish
    (such as coley, whiting or pollack)

450 g (1 lb) mashed potato

2 tablespoons chopped parsley

salt

freshly ground black pepper

225 g (8 oz) Cheddar cheese, grated

2 eggs, beaten

sesame seeds or porridge oats, to coat

lemon wedges, to serve

Preparation time: 25 minutes, plus
chilling
Cooking time: about 20 minutes

1. Fork the flaked fish into the mashed
potato. Add the chopped parsley and
season to taste with salt and pepper.
2. Scoop out a large spoonful, and mould
into a ball shape in your hand (flour your
hands first if the mixture is sticky). Press a
few small spoonfuls of grated cheese into
the middle of each ball. Flatten into a
burger shape and continue until all the
mixture has been used.
3. Dip the burgers in the beaten egg and
coat in sesame seeds or porridge oats.
4. Chill for 30 minutes then shallow fry,
bake or grill and serve with lemon wedges,
grilled tomatoes and a selection of green
vegetables or a salad.

ABOVE RIGHT: Fish and sorrel omelette
BELOW RIGHT: Cheesey fish burgers

SEAFOOD PILAU

SERVES 6-8

1 clove garlic, crushed
1 medium onion, peeled and finely chopped
1 tablespoon vegetable oil
75 g (3 oz) butter
450 g (1 lb) long-grain rice
600 ml (1 pint) fish stock (see page 139)
600 ml (1 pint) boiling water
salt
freshly ground black pepper
175 g (6 oz) button mushrooms, wiped and
   finely sliced
225 g (8 oz) petit pois
1×184 g (6½ oz) can pimentos, chopped
450 g (1 lb) firm white fish (such as cod,
   hake or eel) cooked and flaked, or cut into
   bite-sized pieces
225 g (8 oz) peeled cooked prawns
225 g (8 oz) canned or fresh mussels
4 tablespoons chopped parsley

To garnish:
1 whole, cooked, unpeeled prawn
bay leaves

Preparation time: 15 minutes
Cooking time: about 25 minutes

A basic pilau is a quick, simple and attractive base for almost any kind of seafood. It is especially attractive to children, and useful too for using up left-over cooked fish. You could also serve the pilau chilled with a salad – toss a few seedless white grapes and fresh green herbs into the pilau and serve on a bed of Chinese leaves with a light mayonnaise dressing.

1. In a large, heavy frying or sauté pan, soften the garlic and onion in the oil and 25 g (1 oz) of the butter until pale and transparent, then stir in the rice until it is glistening and hot.
2. Pour in the stock and boiling water, bring up to just simmering point. Season with salt and pepper and give a gentle stir or two, cover and leave to cook gently for about 15 minutes.
3. Meanwhile, melt the remaining butter in another pan and gently cook the mushrooms – remove with a slotted spoon and reserve.
4. When the rice is almost cooked, add the petit pois and pimentos. At this stage you may need to add a little more liquid – use more stock, boiling water or white wine.
5. Cook for a further 2-3 minutes, then tip in the seafood and mushrooms and carefully turn the pilau until all is well incorporated and hot – be careful not to overcook at this stage.
6. Scatter the chopped parsley over the pilau, garnish with the whole prawn and bay leaves and take the pan straight to the table to serve. A tossed green salad makes a good accompaniment to this dish.

LEFT: Seafood pilau

JACKET POTATOES

The renewed popularity of potatoes after years of being wrongly labelled as fattening is very welcome. There are many varieties of potato to choose from and potatoes and fish are wonderful partners, providing nutritious and balanced meals for everyone – as simple or elaborate as you like. You can cook jacket potatoes very quickly in the microwave, which makes them an ideal snack or supper – especially for children – or a quick main meal served with green vegetables or a salad. Each filling makes enough for 4 large potatoes. Bake the potatoes in a preheated, moderately hot oven, 200°C, 400°F, Gas Mark 6 for about 1 hour or alternatively bake them at full power in the microwave for about 20 minutes.

COTTAGE CHEESE, COD AND KIPPER FILLING

2 tablespoons sunflower seeds
a little oil
100 g (4 oz) cod, cooked and flaked
100 g (4 oz) kipper fillet, cooked, skinned
  and cut into thin strips
225 g (8 oz) cottage cheese
salt
freshly ground black pepper
2 tablespoons chopped parsley, to garnish

Preparation time: 10 minutes
Cooking time: 5 minutes

1. Sauté the sunflower seeds in a little oil.
2. Mix together the cod, kipper and cottage cheese, season to taste with salt and pepper and use to fill the cooked potatoes.
3. Garnish the potatoes with the sunflower seeds and parsley.

SHRIMP AND SPRING ONION FILLING

225 g (8 oz) peeled cooked shrimps
150 ml (¼ pint) soured cream
150 ml (¼ pint) plain unsweetened yogurt
a few drops of Tabasco sauce
4 spring onions, trimmed and finely
  chopped
salt
pinch of freshly ground black pepper
1 spring onion, trimmed and finely chopped,
  to garnish

Preparation time: 10 minutes

1. When the potatoes are cooked, remove them from the oven and cut them almost in half lengthways and crossways to form a criss-cross in the centre of the potato.
2. Combine the shrimps, soured cream, yogurt and a few drops of Tabasco sauce together in a bowl. Then heap the mixture into the centre of the potatoes.
3. Garnish the potatoes with chopped spring onion.
4. Serve the potatoes with a selection of salads.

FAR RIGHT: Jacket potato with cottage cheese, cod and kipper filling
RIGHT: Jacket potato with shrimp and spring onion filling

SMOKED HADDOCK AND LEEK FLAN

SERVES 4-6
2 quantities shortcrust pastry (see page 12)
50 g (2 oz) butter
50 g (2 oz) plain flour
600 ml (1 pint) milk
salt
freshly ground black pepper
350 g (12 oz) smoked haddock, flaked
450 g (1 lb) leeks, trimmed and finely chopped
50 g (2 oz) Gruyère or Cheddar cheese, grated
finely chopped green part of the leeks, to garnish

Preparation time: 30 minutes
Cooking time: about 45 minutes
Oven: 200°C, 400°F, Gas Mark 6

This is a very quick flan to make. In a flash you have a lovely lunch or snack which can be served with a crisp green salad and crunchy bread, or jacket potatoes.

1. Use the pastry to line a 25 cm (10 inch) flan tin or dish. Prick the base with a fork, line with foil, fill with beans and bake blind in a preheated oven for 10 minutes. Remove the foil and beans and return to the oven for 2-3 minutes.
2. Melt the butter in a saucepan and stir in the flour, cook for a few minutes. Gradually add the milk and bring gently up to simmering point, whisking with a balloon whisk or stirring continuously with a wooden spoon as it thickens.
3. Continue to simmer for 1-2 minutes, until smooth and creamy, then season with salt and pepper.

4. Remove from the heat, and fold in the flaked smoked haddock and finely chopped raw leeks.
5. Pour into the flan case, top with the grated cheese and return to the oven for 20 minutes.
6. Serve immediately, garnished with the finely chopped green part of the leeks.

FISH CROQUETTES

450 g (1 lb) cooked white fish fillets, skinned (such as cod, hake, coley or brill)
450 g (1 lb) cooked potato, mashed
1 bulb fennel, trimmed and finely chopped
2 tablespoons roughly chopped parsley
25 g (1 oz) soft margarine
1 egg (size 1), beaten
pinch of salt
pinch of freshly ground black pepper
100 g (4 oz) sesame seeds
a little vegetable oil (optional)

Preparation time: 25 minutes, plus chilling
Cooking time: about 12 minutes
Oven: 220°C, 420°F, Gas Mark 7

FAR LEFT: Smoked haddock and leek flan
LEFT: Fish croquettes

I love the crunchy texture of the sesame coating on these croquettes, but you could substitute toasted breadcrumbs if you prefer. They are quickly prepared using a food processor, and ideal for freezing for up to 6 months. They can be baked directly from the freezer.

1. Flake the fish, making sure there are no bones. Place in a bowl with the mashed potato, chopped fennel, parsley and margarine. Blend with a fork until all the ingredients are well mashed, adding the beaten egg to bind, if necessary.
2. Transfer the mixture to a mixing bowl, season to taste with salt and pepper and place in a refrigerator. Chill for about 1 hour until nice and firm to handle.
3. Shape the mixture into croquettes and, on a large plate, roll each croquette carefully in sesame seeds until well coated.

4. The croquettes can now be placed on a lightly greased baking tray and baked in a preheated oven for about 12 minutes, turning once during the cooking time.
5. Serve immediately with a salad or steamed strips of carrot, parsnip and spring onion, and a spoonful of fresh tomato sauce (see page 140).

FISH PASTIES

2 quantities shortcrust pastry (see page 12)
wholemeal flour, for dusting
450 g (1 lb) potatoes, peeled and finely
* sliced*
1 medium onion or 2 leeks, peeled or
* trimmed and finely sliced*
1 tablespoon freshly chopped parsley
salt
freshly ground black pepper
1 tablespoon single cream
350 g (12 oz) white fish fillets, skinned and
* cut into bite-sized pieces*
100 g (4 oz) smoked salmon scraps or
* smoked fish fillet, cut into bite-sized pieces*
1 egg, beaten, for glazing

Preparation time: 35 minutes
Cooking time: 40-55 minutes
Oven: 220°C, 420°F, Gas Mark 7; then
180°C, 350°F, Gas Mark 4

These are excellent for picnics, *al fresco* suppers, packed lunches or – dare I suggest it – a meal in front of the television! Wrap in thick paper napkins for family and friends to eat in their hands.

1. Roll out the pastry on a board dusted with wholemeal flour (this gives a lovely speckled texture to the finished pastry).
2. Cut round a large side plate or small dinner plate to make 4 rounds.
3. In a large bowl toss together the prepared vegetables, herbs, season with salt and pepper and moisten with the cream. Mix together using your fingers.
4. Heap 2-3 tablespoons of this mixture into the centre of each pastry round. Then top with the white and smoked fish. The filling should be generous, if you have too little mixture it will shrink during cooking and your pasty will be half hollow.
5. Bring both sides of the pastry up to the centre, and crimp the edges.

6. Using a fish slice, carefully transfer the pasties to a lightly greased baking tray.
7. Brush the pasties with the beaten egg and bake in a preheated oven for 10-15 minutes to cook the pastry. Then reduce the heat and continue to bake for about 30 minutes, until the filling has cooked deliciously in its own juices. Test that the filling is cooked with a skewer.
8. Serve immediately or wrap in foil and put in an insulated picnic bag for a picnic outing or barbecue.

KEDGEREE

450 g (1 lb) smoked haddock fillets
milk, for poaching
1 small onion or 2-3 spring onions, peeled or
* trimmed and finely chopped*
50 g (2 oz) butter
225 g (8 oz) cooked long-grain rice
4 hard-boiled eggs, chopped
4 tablespoons freshly chopped parsley
salt
freshly ground black pepper

To garnish:
spring onion tassels
hard-boiled egg wedges

Preparation time: 10 minutes
Cooking time: about 15 minutes

Lovely for breakfast – or supper. This simple, tasty dish is good with chutney or tomato relish.

1. Place the haddock in a pan and add milk to cover. Poach the haddock in the milk for 10-15 minutes. Lift off and discard the skin and flake the flesh. Reserve the milk.
2. Cook the onion or spring onions in the butter, add the rice and stir as it gently heats through.
3. Add the flaked haddock, taking care not to break up the flesh too much, carefully stir in the parsley and the reserved milk and then add the hard-boiled eggs. Season to taste with salt and pepper.
4. Garnish with spring onion tassels and wedges of hard-boiled egg.

ABOVE RIGHT: Fish pasties
BELOW RIGHT: Kedgeree

SMOKED MACKEREL AND COTTAGE CHEESE FLAN

2 quantities shortcrust pastry (see page 12)
225 g (8 oz) smoked mackerel fillets
2 eggs
225 g (8 oz) cottage cheese
2 tomatoes, chopped
salt
freshly ground black pepper

To garnish:
cherry tomatoes
coriander sprigs

Preparation time: 30 minutes
Cooking time: 35-40 minutes
Oven: 200°C, 400°F, Gas Mark 6; then:
180°C, 350°F, Gas Mark 4

A very simple and quick recipe. Substitute smoked salmon, trout, or kipper fillets for the smoked mackerel if you wish. Serve it hot or cold with a crisp green salad.

1. Use the pastry to line a 20 cm (8 inch) flan tin or dish. Prick the base with a fork and bake blind in a preheated oven for 10 minutes. Remove the foil and beans and return to the oven for 2-3 minutes.
2. Remove the skin from the smoked mackerel fillets and flake or slice the flesh into small pieces.

3. In a mixing bowl, beat the eggs and combine with the cottage cheese, fish and chopped tomatoes. Season to taste with salt and pepper.
4. Put this mixture into the pre-baked flan case and bake in a preheated oven for about 25 minutes.
5. Serve hot or cold garnished with cherry tomatoes and sprigs of coriander.

HERRINGS IN OATMEAL

plain flour, for dusting
salt
freshly ground black pepper
4 whole herrings, filleted
100 g (4 oz) porridge oats
1 teaspoon dried mustard powder
2-3 eggs, beaten
oil, for shallow frying
chives, to garnish

Preparation time: 15 minutes
Cooking time: about 10 minutes

ABOVE LEFT: Smoked mackerel and cottage cheese flan
BELOW LEFT: Herrings in oatmeal

This is a traditional dish from Scotland which makes a very tasty supper, though it is also a marvellous meal at anytime.

1. Season the flour with salt and pepper and use to dust the herrings.
2. Mix the porridge oats and mustard powder together. Dip the fish into the beaten eggs and then coat with the oat mixture.
3. Heat the oil in a large frying pan and shallow fry the herrings until golden brown in colour, about 5 minutes each side, turning once.
4. Drain well on paper towels, garnish with chives and serve piping hot with thin slices of brown bread and butter.

BARBECUES AND SALADS

What could be more delightful for every type of occasion – summer lunches, children's parties, picnics and even bonfire night, than a barbecue sizzling with a feast of seafood. Fish and shellfish are the ideal barbecue food. The huge variety of fish and shellfish available can be combined with many different ingredients – simple or exotic – to produce a visual delight of dishes.

Barbecued scallops (see page 106)

COD KEBABS WITH BARBECUE SAUCE

750 g (1½ lb) cod steaks
12 sprigs of rosemary
12-16 button mushrooms, wiped and stalks
  removed

Marinade:
2 teaspoons prepared mustard
4 teaspoons Worcestershire sauce
4 tablespoons red wine vinegar
4 tablespoons olive or sunflower oil
4 tablespoons tomato ketchup

Preparation time: 15 minutes, plus marinating
Cooking time: about 5 minutes

1. Remove the skin and bones from the cod and cut into chunks. Place in a glass or earthenware bowl.
2. Combine the marinade ingredients, pour over the cod and leave to marinate for 20 minutes turning occasionally.
3. Make sure the barbecue is hot. Oil the kebab skewers and thread on the chunks of cod interspersed with the rosemary and mushrooms.
4. Grill the kebabs over the barbecue or under the grill, turning and basting with the marinade.
5. Serve immediately with a crisp green salad, and pour the remaining marinade over the kebabs.

If you are having a barbecue party why not vary these kebabs by using a selection of brightly coloured vegetables; choose from chunks of courgette, button onions, cherry tomatoes, squares of red, green or yellow pepper and use a selection of different herbs such as bay and sage leaves.

BARBECUED SCALLOPS

SERVES 3-4
12 prepared scallops, halved
24 rashers streaky bacon
lemon wedges
bay leaves
lemon wedges, to serve

Preparation time: 10 minutes
Cooking time: about 3 minutes

1. Wrap each piece of scallop in a rasher of bacon and thread onto an oiled skewer, alternating with wedges of lemon and bay leaves.
2. Cook on the barbecue or under the grill for about 3 minutes, turning regularly, until the bacon is crisp and brown.
3. Serve with lemon wedges.

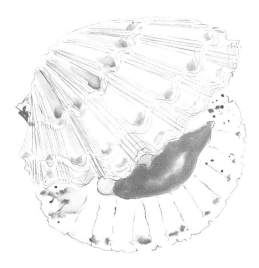

ABOVE RIGHT: Cod kebabs with barbecue sauce
BELOW RIGHT: Barbecued scallops

BARBECUED HAKE WITH COURGETTE PARCELS

4 hake cutlets, about 2.5 cm (1 inch) thick
4 medium-large courgettes
salt
freshly ground black pepper
100 g (4 oz) blanched almonds, slivered
25 g (1 oz) butter
fennel sprigs, to garnish

Marinade:
4 tablespoons olive oil
2 tablespoons orange juice
2 tablespoons lemon juice
pinch of salt
5 black peppercorns, bruised
1 shallot, peeled and finely chopped
1 tablespoon finely chopped fennel

Preparation time: 25 minutes, plus marinating
Cooking time: about 15 minutes

A lovely combination of taste and texture.

1. First combine the marinade ingredients. Wash the hake cutlets and pat dry with paper towels. Pour the marinade over the hake and leave to marinate for 1-1½ hours, turning occasionally.
2. Meanwhile, lightly butter 4 large pieces of foil. Thinly slice the courgettes, and put a serving onto each piece of foil. Season lightly with salt and pepper, sprinkle over a few slivered almonds and add a tiny dot of butter to each piece of foil.
3. Wrap up the foil to form parcels and place on the barbecue.
4. As soon as you hear the courgettes hissing or sizzling, put the hake cutlets on the oiled grid of the barbecue and, basting frequently with the marinade, cook for a few minutes on each side.
5. Put the foil parcels on individual plates, peel back to reveal the courgettes in their own juices, and place a cooked hake cutlet alongside.
6. Garnish with sprigs of fennel and serve with a potato salad.

LEFT: Barbecued hake with courgette parcels

MARINATED MONKFISH KEBABS

SERVES 4-6
about 750 g-1 kg (1½-2 lb) monkfish
12-16 bay leaves
12 whole, cooked, unpeeled prawns
1 large mango
1 galen melon

Marinade:
1 small onion or shallot, peeled
4-8 tablespoons orange juice
4-8 tablespoons lemon juice
equal quantity of olive oil to the citrus juice
salt
freshly ground black pepper
2 teaspoons crushed cardamom seeds

Preparation time: 15 minutes, plus marinating
Cooking time: about 5 minutes

The fresh chilled taste of the mango and galen melon with the hot kebabs is a wonderful combination.

1. Cut the monkfish flesh into chunky cubes and place in a glass or earthenware bowl large enough to hold the marinade.
2. Make the marinade. Chop the onion or shallot finely and add the orange and lemon juice, the same quantity of olive oil, pinch each of salt and pepper, and the crushed cardamom seeds. Give the marinade a stir, and pour over the cubes of monkfish – leave to marinate in a cool place for 2 hours.

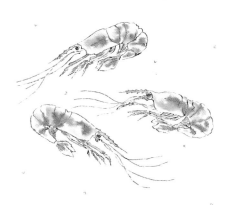

3. Thread 4 oiled skewers alternately with the marinated monkfish, bay leaves and whole, unpeeled prawns.
4. Place the monkfish kebabs over the barbecue fire or under a preheated hot grill, turning them slowly and basting all the time with the marinade whilst cooking. Reserve a little of the marinade and use as a dressing for an accompanying green salad, if desired.
5. Arrange the kebabs on a plate with slices of mango and galen melon.
6. Serve the kebabs with a green salad.

RIGHT: Marinated monkfish kebabs

MONKFISH AND AVOCADO SALAD

SERVES 4-6

750 g (1½ lb) monkfish, skinned and boned

300 ml (½ pint) fish stock (see page 139) or dry white wine

4 courgettes, grated or shredded

2 ripe avocados, peeled and sliced

squeeze of fresh lemon juice

2 celery sticks, trimmed and very finely sliced

225 g (8 oz) seedless grapes

4 tablespoons mayonnaise (see page 140)

4 tablespoons fromage blanc or plain unsweetened yogurt

3-4 teaspoons tomato purée

pinch of cayenne

celery leaves, to garnish

Preparation time: 30 minutes

Cooking time: about 10 minutes

The delicate shades of pale pink and pale green make an elegant presentation for this summer salad.

1. Cut the monkfish into medallions and poach in the stock or wine for about 5 minutes. Transfer with a slotted spoon to a cool dish or plate and set aside.

2. Reserve 1 tablespoon of the cooking liquid for the sauce, and keep the remaining liquid for a soup or stew – it can even be frozen for future use.

3. On a large oval or round serving plate or platter, make a border around the rim with the grated or shredded courgettes, then inside this border arrange the avocado slices so that they are overlapping. Sprinkle with lemon juice.

4. In a bowl, combine the monkfish, celery and grapes.

5. Mix together the mayonnaise, fromage blanc or yogurt, tomato purée, cayenne and add a tiny squeeze of lemon juice to

sharpen. Stir in 1 tablespoon of the cooled cooking liquid to thin down the sauce and add flavour.

6. Put the fish, celery and grape mixture into the sauce and then heap into the centre of the salad arrangement.

7. Garnish with celery leaves and serve with a plate of thinly sliced fresh tomatoes and fresh bread rolls.

LEFT: Monkfish and avocado salad

KIPPER, APPLE AND ONION SALAD

SERVES 2-3
225 g (8 oz) cooked kipper fillets
2 red dessert apples
1 small onion, peeled
4 tablespoons double cream
4 tablespoons plain unsweetened yogurt
squeeze of fresh lemon juice
salt
freshly ground black pepper
Chinese leaves, to serve

To garnish:
apple slices
mint sprigs

Preparation time: 20 minutes

1. Skin the kipper fillets, and flake the fish into chunks.
2. Core the apples (leaving the skin on) and cut into small chunks. Slice the onion into very thin half rounds. There should be more or less equal quantities of these 3 ingredients, but cut down a little on the onion if it is strong.
3. Combine the cream and yogurt together, add a squeeze of lemon juice to taste and season with salt and pepper. Mix into the kipper, apple and onion mixture.
4. Arrange 4 large Chinese leaves on a platter, and heap the mixture into the cradle of each leaf.
5. Garnish with apple slices and sprigs of mint.

SALAD MONTE CRISTO

450 g (1 lb) cod fillet, skinned and cubed
150 ml (¼ pint) court bouillon (see page 139)
2 dessert pears, cut into chunks
50 g (2 oz) walnut pieces
1 bunch watercress
½ head of frisée, roughly chopped
salt
freshly ground black pepper
tarragon sprigs, to garnish

Dressing:
1 clove garlic, crushed
1 tablespoon white wine vinegar
5 tablespoons olive oil
2 tablespoons finely chopped fresh tarragon

Preparation time: 20 minutes
Cooking time: 4-5 minutes

1. Poach the cubed cod in the court bouillon for 4-5 minutes. Drain the cod, leave to cool then chill in the refrigerator.
2. Place the chilled fish in a large bowl and mix with the remaining ingredients.

3. To make the dressing, put all the ingredients in a screw-top jar and shake well to combine.
4. Pour the dressing over the salad and serve garnished with sprigs of tarragon.

ABOVE RIGHT: Kipper, apple and onion salad
BELOW RIGHT: Salad Monte Cristo

HARICOT BEAN AND FISH SALAD

SERVES 4-6

225 g (8 oz) haricot beans
salt
freshly ground black pepper
vinaigrette dressing (see page 141)
450 g (1 lb) cooked white fish, flaked
1 shallot or 4 spring onions, peeled or
  trimmed
2 dessert apples
1 orange
2-3 tablespoons chopped fresh herbs, as
  available
100 g (4 oz) black olives, pitted
4 tomatoes, peeled and quartered
2 celery sticks, trimmed and finely sliced
1 crisp lettuce or chicory, to serve

Preparation time: 25 minutes, plus
soaking overnight
Cooking time: 2-3 hours

Use any firm-fleshed white fish for this
salad; whiting is particularly good.

1. Cover the haricot beans with water and
soak overnight.
2. Drain the beans, cover again with water,
then simmer for 2-3 hours in a covered
pan until tender.
3. Drain, season with salt and pepper (do
not add any salt until the beans have been
cooked as otherwise they will become
tough) and while the beans are still hot,
toss them in the vinaigrette dressing.
4. Flake the fish, slice the shallot or spring
onions, core the apples and chop into tiny
chunks, leaving the skin on.
5. Peel, segment and chop the orange,
keeping the juice.
6. Combine all the ingredients together,
including the reserved orange juice, in
a large bowl and taste and adjust the
seasoning, if necessary.
7. Arrange the salad on a bed of crisp
lettuce or chicory. Serve with rye bread or
wholemeal rolls.

LEFT: Haricot bean and fish salad

SKATE SALAD WITH RUSSIAN DRESSING

2 skate wings
600 ml (1 pint) court bouillon (see page 139)
1 crisp lettuce, shredded
1 bunch watercress, trimmed
1 cucumber, diced
4 celery sticks, trimmed and sliced
1 bunch spring onions, trimmed and sliced
  lengthways, including the green part
100 g (4 oz) button mushrooms, wiped and
  thinly sliced
chopped fresh herbs, to garnish

Dressing:
175 ml (6 fl oz) tomato juice
4 tablespoons olive oil
4 tablespoons lemon juice
1 small onion, peeled and chopped
1 tablespoon clear honey
pinch of salt
pinch of freshly ground black pepper
1 teaspoon paprika
1 clove garlic, crushed

Preparation time: 25 minutes, plus
chilling
Cooking time: about 10 minutes

1. Poach the skate wings in the court bouillon, remove the skate from the pan and leave to cool.
2. Thoroughly drain the fish, remove the skin, and shred the flesh from the wings. Reserve the stock for another dish.
3. Make up a salad using the shredded lettuce, watercress, cucumber, celery, spring onions and mushrooms, and leave to chill in the refrigerator while preparing the dressing.

4. Blend the ingredients for the dressing in a food processor or blender.
5. Combine the shredded skate and chilled salad ingredients, pour in the prepared dressing and toss well.
6. Serve the chilled salad in a salad bowl. Sprinkle over fresh herbs to garnish.

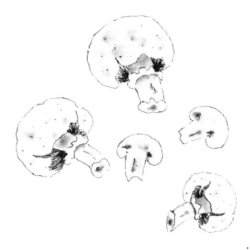

LOBSTER SALAD WITH TARRAGON SAUCE

1 lobster or crawfish, weighing 750 g (1½ lb)
2 cucumbers
½ teaspoon salt
1 teaspoon sugar
1-2 tablespoons tarragon vinegar
100 g (4 oz) petit pois
200 g (7 oz) mayonnaise
200 g (7 oz) plain unsweetened yogurt
2-3 sprigs fresh tarragon, chopped
about 6 tablespoons fish stock (see page 139)
1 crisp lettuce
tarragon sprigs, to garnish

Preparation time: 35 minutes
Cooking time: 2-3 minutes

1. Extract the meat from the lobster (see page 138).
2. Peel and seed the cucumbers then slice into matchstick strips. Toss them in a basin with a marinade of salt, sugar and vinegar and leave in a cool place for 1 hour.
3. Blanch the petit pois in boiling salted water for 2-3 minutes, drain and cool.
4. Combine the mayonnaise, yogurt and chopped tarragon – then carefully stir in about 6 tablespoons of fish stock, to make a smooth consistency.
5. Shred the lettuce and use to make a bed on a platter.
6. Cut the lobster meat into chunky slices

and pile on top of the lettuce. Mix the petit pois with the rinsed, drained cucumber and arrange around the edge of the dish.
7. Pour over the sauce and garnish with sprigs of fresh tarragon.

ABOVE RIGHT: Skate salad with Russian dressing
BELOW RIGHT: Lobster salad with tarragon sauce

TANGY FISH SALAD

SERVES 6-8
750 g (1½ lb) smoked haddock fillets,
  skinned
40 g (1½ oz) butter
300 ml (½ pint) plain unsweetened yogurt
grated rind of 1 lemon
2 celery sticks, trimmed and chopped
1 red dessert apple, cored and diced
25 g (1 oz) walnuts, coarsely chopped
salt
freshly ground black pepper
lettuce leaves, to serve (optional)

Preparation time: 25 minutes, plus
chilling
Cooking time: about 5 minutes

1. Cut the fish into 1 cm (½ inch) cubes.
2. Melt the butter in a large frying pan and gently cook the fish for a few minutes on either side. Drain, leave to cool then chill for 2 hours.

3. Mix the remaining ingredients together and add to the cubed haddock. Season with salt and pepper to taste. Serve on a bed of lettuce leaves or alternatively in individual glasses as a starter.

PINK GRAPEFRUIT AND SHELLFISH SALAD

2 pink grapefruit
1 crisp lettuce, shredded
½ cucumber, peeled, seeded and diced
225 g (8 oz) crab meat, flaked
175 g (6 oz) peeled cooked prawns
1 tablespoon plain unsweetened yogurt
4 tablespoons mayonnaise (see page 140)
squeeze of fresh lemon or lime juice
salt
freshly ground black pepper

To garnish:
lime twists
chervil sprigs
julienne strips of lime rind

Preparation time: 25 minutes

LEFT: Tangy fish salad
BELOW LEFT: Pink grapefruit and shellfish salad

This salad looks particularly attractive if the grapefruit shells are cut in a zig-zag pattern around the top edge before being filled. If pink grapefruit is unavailable use normal grapefruit

1. Slice the grapefruit in half, crosswise, and scoop out the segments. Reserve the juice and the grapefruit shells.
2. Chop the grapefruit segments and combine with half the shredded lettuce, the diced cucumber, the flaked crab meat and the prawns.
3. Beat the yogurt into the mayonnaise, and add a teaspoon of the reserved grapefruit juice, and a squeeze of lemon or lime juice. Season to taste with salt and pepper.
4. Line the hollowed grapefruit halves with the remaining lettuce and heap in the seafood salad.
5. Spoon the mayonnaise dressing over the salad in the grapefruit shells and garnish

with twists of lime, sprigs of chervil and julienne strips of lime rind.

CEVICHE

8 large fresh prepared scallops, or 450 g
  (1 lb) monkfish, skinned and boned
12-16 tablespoons fresh lemon juice
6 tablespoons fresh lime juice
coriander sprigs, to garnish

Salad:
4 tomatoes, quartered
1 green pepper, cored, seeded and chopped
1 bunch spring onions, trimmed and sliced
  lengthways
1 avocado, peeled, stoned and sliced
bunch of coarsely chopped parsley or chervil

Dressing:
1 clove garlic, crushed
150 ml (¼ pint) olive oil
pinch of salt
pinch of freshly ground black pepper
6 drops of Tabasco sauce

Preparation time: 25 minutes, plus
marinating and chilling

This is a dish of raw fish which is
marinated in citrus juices. The marinade
has a similar effect on the flesh as cooking.
However, if you feel wary of the idea of
raw fish, you could scald the fish in boiling
water before preparing it, but the texture
will be different. It is most important to
use only very fresh fish for this dish.

1. Cut each scallop into 2-3 thick slices, or
slice the monkfish into medallions.
2. Pour over a mixture of the lemon juice
and lime juice, cover and leave to marinate
in the refrigerator for 4-6 hours.
3. Make the dressing. Put all the
ingredients in a screw-top jar, tighten the
lid and shake well to combine.
4. Mix all the salad ingredients together
carefully, and toss in the dressing – chill in
the refrigerator for about 30 minutes.
5. Drain the marinade juices from the fish,
and combine the fish with the salad.
6. Garnish with sprigs of coriander.

Ceviche is a very popular dish in South America
and the South Pacific. The addition of avocado is
a typically Mexican idea, while in the Pacific
Islands fresh coconut milk is added towards the
end of the preparation. Ceviche is perfect to serve
as a more unusual dinner party starter or at a
light luncheon; other fish such as cod, salmon and
tuna can also be used.

RIGHT: Ceviche

RECIPE AND MENU PLANNER

BUFFET PARTY

Taramasalata: page 10

Seafood Puffs: page 10

Fish Tartlets: page 12

Smoked Mackerel Pâté: page 15

Salad Monte Cristo: page 114

Haricot Bean and Fish Salad: page 117

Skate Salad with Russian Dressing: page 118

QUICK DISHES

Smoked Mackerel with Stir-Fried Vegetables: page 46

Sole with Gherkin Sauce: page 58

Fettuccine alla Trota: page 88

Fish and Sorrel Omelette: page 92

Herrings in Oatmeal: page 103

Kipper, Apple and Onion Salad: page 114

Tangy Fish Salad: page 121

FAMILY MEALS

Cod Steaks à la Grecque: page 38

Seafish Aubergines: page 41

Haddock in a Curry Sauce: page 45

Hake Florentine: page 42

Fish Cobbler: page 53

Seafood Pancakes: page 57

Fish, Courgette and Brown Rice Bake: page 58

Crispy Fish Hotpot: page 61

DINNER PARTY DISHES

Layered Fish Terrine: page 8

Trout with Almonds: page 83

Crab and Avocado Mousse: page 16

Red Mullet with Orange and Fennel: page 68

Moules à la Marinière: page 16

Salmon with Three Sauces: page 72

Lobster Bisque: page 27

Sole Bonne Femme: page 76

Chilled Avocado and Smoked Haddock Soup: page 31

Lobster Thermidor: page 84

Grilled Oysters with Garlic Butter: page 19

Skate in Orange and Cider Sauce: page 80

FOOD FACTS

A GUIDE TO FISH

There are about sixty species of fish and shellfish on sale in Britain.

The families of fish can most easily be categorized as belonging to one of the following groups:

1. Pelagic: Fish which live in large groups or shoals and frequent the middle and surface layers of the seas, such as herring and mackerel. Trawlers catch these fish as they feed upon plankton and the small crustacea and organisms which drift about in the upper layers of the sea.

2. Demersal: These are bottom fish, which live on or near the sea bed, and include cod and all its relations (such as haddock and hake) and flat fish such as plaice and turbot.

3. Shellfish: In two general groups: *Molluscs* are shellfish with shells or mantles which have no limbs – such as oysters, clams, mussels, cockles and winkles. They are usually collected by hand. *Crustaceans* are shellfish with limbs such as lobsters, crawfish, crayfish, prawns, shrimps or crabs. There is always confusion between prawns and shrimps – prawns are slightly larger than shrimps, and shrimps have longer antennae; but they are more or less the same animal, in taste and shape. To add to the confusion, Americans call the British prawns shrimps – and the Dublin Bay prawn is really a type of lobster, also known as scampi or langoustine! *Crawfish* is similar in size and taste to lobster but does not have main claws, whereas *crayfish* is a smaller freshwater crustacean. One of the fascinations about

seafood is that our technological world has not been able to standardize and 'package' the harvest of the sea.

Fish can also be classified in groups of:
a. Round white fish
b. Flat white fish
c. Oily fish
d. Shellfish – crustaceans and molluscs
e. Cartilaginous fish – for example, monkfish, huss and skate.

TYPES OF FISH AND SHELLFISH

Bass (Sea Bass): is sometimes known as salmon bass although it does not belong to the salmon family. It is a handsome silvery fish, with superb lean white flesh. It is good steamed or baked whole, and steaks or cutlets are excellent when grilled or barbecued.

Brill: a flat fish of good flavour, which is best cooked on the bone, using recipes also suitable for turbot.

Cod: is a marvellously versatile fish with a high nutritional value, which can be cooked by any method. The roe is good grilled and served with toast, and smoked cod's roe is used for making taramasalata.

Coley: also known as saithe and coalfish, a member of the cod family, tough with darker coloured flesh which turns white when cooked. It is usually sold in fillets and can be used for any recipe calling · for cod or haddock.

Conger Eel: gaining in popularity again, this marine eel has a good strong flavour and firm flesh, making it ideal for braises and pies. Smoked conger eel makes a slightly different though delicious starter or salad.

Crab: of the many species of crab around our shores, the large common crab is the one we usually see on sale in Britain. But spider crab and the blue swimming crabs are worth looking for when on holiday – they can be cooked and used in the same way as the common crab.

Crawfish: also known as spiny lobster. The crawfish is a 'lobster red' colour *before* it is cooked, whereas live lobster is a beautiful, slatey-blue colour and turns red only after boiling. It differs from lobster in that it does not have two main claws.

Dab: available whole or filleted, dab is a good economical flat fish which can be used in many recipes calling for an inexpensive flat fish.

Haddock: a member of the cod family and considered by many to be superior. It has a distinctive thumb print on each side, supposedly representing the mark of the finger and thumb of St Peter. The roe is a great delicacy and is very popular in France.

Hake: is a member of the cod family. It has very white, firm flesh, is easily boned and can be bought whole or in fillets and cutlets. It can be used for most white fish recipes.

Halibut: the largest of all the flat fish – the maximum length of a halibut can be 3 metres (10 feet). Fillets or steaks of halibut should be cooked in lightly buttered foil, brushed with an oil-based marinade or a little melted savoury butter, as the flesh tends to be dry. Chicken halibut (the young, smaller fish) can be cooked like sole.

Herring: the name herring comes from the Teutonic word 'Heer' meaning army. This is very appropriate as a shoal of these beautiful fish, with their streamlined bodies built for speed, may cover a vast area and contain many thousands, if not millions, of fish! Herring is a very nutritious fish and is a particularly rich source of protein, fat, iodine and vitimins A and D. Oily fish like herring are excellent to grill or barbecue.

Huss: also known as dogfish, flake or rigg, is a cartilaginous (i.e. non-bony) fish and is, in fact, a species of shark. It is a good all-purpose fish, usually bought skinned. In the past their tough skins were used for polishing wood and alabaster!

John Dory: this is an extraordinary fish to behold, and you can carry it like a 'handbag,' which is the best way to pick one up and avoid the very sharp spines – there is a ridge which forms a sort of handle in the upper curve of the fish. Like haddock, it has the distinctive thumb prints of St Peter. The carcass makes excellent stock when you lift off the lovely firm white fillets, or you can bake or grill it whole. The taste is exceptionally good.

Lobster: live lobster are a beautiful slatey-blue colour, turning to a pinky red when cooked. Their flesh is so succulent and superior in taste that they are often best served with a simple salad and wedges of lemon. They do tend to be expensive but, because of the rich taste and texture, a little of its meat goes a long way.

Mackerel: a brilliant dark greeny-blue back with an irregular pattern of still darker zig-zag lines are the beautiful and familiar features of this versatile and delicious oily fish. Grill it, bake it or souse it for wonderful dishes. Smoked mackerel is very popular and, as with all oily fish, tart fruit sauces are an excellent accompaniment and help offset the richness of the flesh.

Megrim: this rather bland fish will need a little extra flavouring – for instance a piquant marinade or a cheese sauce – as this flat fish can be rather dry and lacking in any distinctive flavour of its own.

Monkfish (Anglerfish): the flesh of monkfish is superb in taste and texture and is faintly reminiscent of lobster. It can be cooked in a variety of ways – poached, baked, stewed, grilled or fried and happily is becoming more widely available in this country. The strange and ugly head of monkfish is rarely seen as only the tail end is sold. Incidentally, the whole tail can be roasted (rather like a leg of lamb) with oil, lemon, garlic and rosemary. Bone it first, or not, as you please. A most wonderfully delicious fish.

Mullet, Grey: the flesh of grey mullet has a beautiful flavour, and is very much under-rated. It can be cooked and served in many ways but is particularly good when stuffed and baked whole. Remember that it needs scaling before cooking.

Mullet, Red: a summer visitor to British waters, and very pretty and welcome it is too! It is a fish valued highly for its taste and appearance and is usually cooked intact to give more flavour: the liver is a delicacy. Grilling or baking are the best cooking methods for the delicate flesh.

Mussels: this shellfish deserves more praise: they are cheap, delicious, versatile and easy to cook. Their flavoursome cooking juices give a lovely flavour to sauces and soups.

Norway Lobster: belongs to the lobster family, and is also known as Dublin Bay prawns, scampi and langoustine. Usually the peeled tail is served lightly battered and shallow fried, skewered and grilled, or in various cold seafood dishes. Dublin Bay prawns with the shells left on look beautiful served in mixed seafood salads and, although a rather fiddly finger food, the meat in the claws is well worth picking out.

Oysters: there are three species of oyster which form the basis of the industry in Britain: the European flat oyster, the Portuguese oyster and, more recently, the Pacific or Japanese oyster. You must be an expert to differentiate between their quality. Oysters are a good source of minerals, particularly zinc. The farming of oysters has brought down the price within the scope of the average household budget when entertaining.

Plaice: has a distinctive orange speckled skin and is a good flat fish when very fresh. Small plaice are best served on the bone. Lift off the thick, white fillets of larger plaice and use in a variety of recipes.

Prawns: the quality and flavour of prawns is as various as the different sizes and species now available – whole 'shell-on', or peeled, raw or cooked, fresh or frozen.

Salmon: a magnificent fish often called the king of the sea. Experts differ in their opinion over the taste of farmed or wild salmon but for most people, salmon is a rather special fish. Smoked salmon and Gravad Lax are often served as a starter.

Scallops and Queens: the white flesh of the scallop, with its pinky-orange coral, is a most tender and tasty meat, as too is the much smaller queen. Both shells (or valves) of the queen are rounded, as compared to the great scallop which has one flat and one rounded shell. Scallops, whether grilled, lightly sautéed, or poached, must always be cooked tenderly and quickly or the flesh may become tough. Queens need the same treatment and are also good to use as a stuffing for other varieties of fish.

Shrimps: the brown shrimp which is commonly found in shallow water around the British coast makes a delightful little mouthful when eaten whole – as they are in France. In Britain, they are traditionally potted in butter.

Skate: wings of skate or ray are easily recognizable. Large wings are cut into portions, and often skinned. The flesh is moist and white to pale pink: the taste and texture is excellent. They are best steamed, poached in stock or wine, or shallow fried.

Sole, Dover: a flat fish of superb quality, the flavour of which should never be masked by too-rich sauces or flavourings. It is best to poach or grill this fish carefully and serve it with wedges of lemon and the minimum of fuss. The Dover sole is actually the only true sole and belongs to a different family to that of the lemon sole, but both fish can be cooked whole or in fillets, and respond to the same cooking methods.

Sole, Lemon: a very good flat fish. It has a lovely flavour and many classic recipes are attributed to lemon sole. It is best grilled or baked on the bone.

Squid: this mollusc has a torpedo-shaped body with a transparent inner shell. It is a cephalopod, which literally means 'head footed' and refers to the way in which the arms and tentacles sprout directly from the head. It is a delicious seafood, and easier to prepare than you might imagine.

Trout: fresh trout, to be grilled, sautéed or poached, is widely available in most fishmongers' and supermarkets. Its mild pleasant flavour responds well to all cooking methods.

Turbot: along with Dover sole this fish has the most exquisite flavour of all the flat fish: the flesh is firm, meaty yet tender and juicy. The head and bones are a rich source of gelatine and are excellent used as a base for stocks and sauces. Steaks or fillets of turbot can be grilled, sautéed or poached and recipes for sole and other flat fish can be used. Chicken turbot is young turbot. It is best cooked whole, on the bone.

Whiting: another member of the cod family, and always in plentiful and cheap supply. Use in all recipes calling for white fish, but bear in mind that the flesh is inclined to be rather dry therefore grilling is better avoided.

Witch: also known as Torbay sole, can be confused with sole. The flavour is good and recipes for other flat fish are interchangeable.

BUYING FRESH FISH

Look for bright eyes, glistening skin and firm flesh. The smell should be pleasingly of the sea – a fresh, salty, brisk kind of smell. Reject dullness, red sunken eyes, limp flesh that retains the imprint of your finger, and a smell that is decidedly unpleasant. The gills (if present) should be bright blood red, and the scales (if present) should be firmly attached. With fillets, the flesh should be even, firm and springy with no discoloration, dents, or slime.

Some people consider that certain types of fish – game fish such as salmon, and grey mullet – improve in flavour if kept intact for up to three days from purchase; and that Dover sole has a better flavour after two or three days. This is a matter of opinion and personal taste. One perk of buying a whole fresh fish, ungutted, is that you may find a nice fresh roe (the roe of grey mullet is used for the true taramasalata) – and some fish, like red mullet, are improved by cooking with the liver still in place. If your fishmonger prepares fillets for you, always ask for the head, tail and trimmings for your stock pan.

Remember that fishmongers will clean, fillet and prepare any fish to your liking. Most will be happy to advise you on good buys, and cooking methods.

CUTS AND FILLETS OF FISH

Cutlets
The cut across the middle back of the fish with a short section of backbone. Not a complete circle (or oval) in contrast to steaks.

Steaks
The slice across and through the thick part of a fish including a short section of backbone. Steaks form an unbroken shape. Steaks from flat fish such as plaice and halibut are oval and sometimes described as cutlets.

Middle Cut
A general term covering a large cut taken from the middle of a round fish.

Fillet
A flat piece of fish cut parallel to the backbone with head, fins and bones removed. Two fillets may be cut from a round fish, such as salmon and two or four from a flat fish, such as sole.

BUYING COOKED SHELLFISH

The shells of cooked shellfish, such as crab and lobster, should be intact: if they are cracked, the flavour and texture of the meat may have been damaged by water during cooking. Cooked shellfish should feel heavy for their size. You soon develop an instinct for selecting a heavy specimen – it just 'feels' good. Cooked shellfish which feel light for their size, or which have soft shells, may have moulted recently and will be in poor condition. Poor quality lobster or crab will contain liquid if the shells are cracked prior to cooking – test by shaking them gently. Freshly cooked prawns and shrimps should be firm to the touch and they should be chilled.

It is well worth the effort of picking out the meat of shellfish yourself – in particular crab. A dressed crab is slightly more expensive to buy and yet once you have tackled the technique of shelling and extracting meat from your first crab it is a skill that is never forgotten and which improves with practice.

BUYING LIVE SHELLFISH

Many people decide that buying and cooking live shellfish or crustaceans is not for them! If that is the case your fishmonger will always have cooked lobsters or crabs for you to buy. If, however, you would like to try your hand at it here are some guidelines.

Make sure your fishmonger sells live shellfish and crustaceans from a reliable source. Better still, if possible, buy direct from a fish market or port as the catch is landed.

With live lobster or crab check that both the main claws are present and that they are packed and sold in moist and cool conditions, and are reasonably lively. Lobster tails should spring back into place when uncurled. The tail of the hen lobster and female crawfish is slightly broader than the tail of the cock lobster and male crawfish: and the hen has slightly more shell around the tailpiece, which protects her eggs or coral. Some people say that all hen lobsters are left-handed and all cocks are right-handed (one of the pair of main claws is always larger than the other). This is not strictly speaking true, so do not depend on this method of selecting lobster and crawfish. There is no difference in the taste of male or female lobsters – the best weight, live, is around 750 g – 1 kg (1½-2 lb) for the tenderest and sweetest flesh. Much larger lobsters should be cheaper per kilogramme or pound and are more suitable if you are doing a 'grand' dish with a special kind of sauce.

When selecting crab, bear in mind that the cock crab has bigger main claws than the hen crab, and will therefore yield more white meat. The hen crab usually has smaller claws, but the brown meat (cream) inside the body will be found in greater quantity and quality than the cream of the male crab. You can easily tell the difference between the hen and the cock by looking at the underside of the body: the shape of the tail flap is round on the hen and pointed on the cock crab.

The shells of live shellfish, such as oysters, clams, scallops and mussels, should remain closed or should shut rapidly when tapped. Again, they should be sold in cool and moist conditions.

Do not recoil from the price of some shellfish – most obviously lobster and crawfish. Catching them is a highly skilled and time-consuming profession, and these shellfish are also seasonal, which is all reflected in the price.

Remember too, that you do not need huge portions as the tender flesh is quite rich and filling.

COOKING LIVE SHELLFISH

There are two ways of cooking live lobster. The first is to plunge the lobster head first into a large pan of boiling salted water. The second which the R.S.P.C.A. recommend is to start the lobster in cold water and bring it slowly to the boil, so that it becomes drowsy and then slowly unconscious.

Lobster, crawfish or crab must be boiled in very salty water – about 175 g (6 oz) salt to 1.75 litres (3 pints) water. You can add a little white wine, vinegar, a bay leaf and bouquet garni if you wish. In general, 10 minutes per 450 g (1 lb) is the recommended cooking time, but if you boil *any* lobster for more than 30 minutes the flesh tends to become rather tough.

Crabs of all sizes can be boiled for 10-12 minutes only, and in my experience this unfailingly produces perfect results. Remember that it is slightly easier to extract the flesh from a crab or lobster when it is still warm.

BUYING FROZEN FISH

There are times when you may choose to buy frozen fish and you can find very good frozen or chilled whole fish or fillets which are of good quality and value.

Here are a few guidelines to bear in mind when buying frozen fish. The packaging should be undamaged and the food should feel hard. Do not buy packages which feel soft or mushy because they have started to thaw and may not be safe to eat. There should be no dull white patches on the fish – this is freezer burn caused by prolonged or incorrect storage. There should be no small white ice crystals, which suggest that the fish has started to thaw and been re-frozen. There should be little 'drip' when thawing and, once thawed, the fish should be firm.

SMOKED FISH

In general, look for the following when shopping for smoked fish.

Smoked fish should have a pleasant smoky smell and a bright and glossy surface. A dull, matt surface suggests that poor quality raw fish was used or that the product was not correctly treated. The fish should be firm to the touch - if it is sticky or soggy the raw fish may have been of low quality, or it may have been under-smoked.
- Undyed smoked kippers are nut brown or yellow brown.
- Undyed finnans are usually pale yellow.
- Dyed kippers are usually red brown.
- Dyed cod and haddock fillets are usually gold yellow.

There are, of course, regional variations in the colours, as many of the firms that produce smoked fish are small family businesses with their own traditional recipes and techniques.

When buying smoked eel, be careful to ensure that it does not look dried up and wrinkled – you want to buy a nice fat, moist specimen.

Smoked trout is gaining in popularity as there are now a good number of trout farms and it is no longer the luxury it used to be.

Smoked mackerel, either whole or in fillets, is always a good buy and can be incorporated in many recipes such as kedgeree and quiche. The natural flavour and oiliness of mackerel make it an ideal fish for smoking because it is these qualities which ensure that the fish remains succulent when smoked.

Prime smoked salmon is a luxury, and you will usually want to buy it only for special occasions. But you can buy lower priced off-cuts and scraps and these are wonderful for all sorts of recipes.

Smoking fish is an ancient method of preserving, now, however, the process and tradition of smoking is retained for the lovely flavour it imparts rather than for preservation.

There are two methods of smoking fish in this country:

a. *Cold smoking.* The fish is cured by smoking at an air temperature not higher than 33°C (92°F) to avoid cooking the flesh. Therefore all cold smoked products, except salmon, must be cooked before they are eaten.

b. *Hot smoking.* The fish is smoked at a higher temperature in order to cook the flesh. Hot smoked products do not require further cooking and are ideal for use in salads and pâtés.

COOKING METHODS

The main rules for cooking fish are:
● Never overcook it – remember, the flesh is naturally tender, if overcooked the flesh will dry out and flake. In general, most fish can be cooked in under 10 minutes.
● Cook fresh fish as soon as possible after buying it.
● To check whether fish is cooked through, test the flesh at its thickest part by piercing with a skewer or sharp knife. When the fish is cooked the flesh will be completely white all the way through and should ease off the bone if unfilleted.
● Serve hot fish dishes straight away – do not keep them warm – and remember that fish will continue cooking when removed from a direct heat.
● If adding salt to the dish do so after cooking as during cooking salt will draw moisture from the fish and can cause it to dry out slightly.
● Always preheat the oven or grill.

POACHING

Using a well-flavoured stock such as court bouillon, fish stock, milk, wine or cider, this is a gentle way to cook whole white fish and large fillets. It is not really suitable for oily varieties of fish, with the exception of salmon.

The technique of poaching is simple but one rule must always be observed – the poaching liquid must NEVER boil. It should quiver and shudder, just short of simmering. A fish kettle is not absolutely essential for whole fish as you can improvise with foil.

Two tips for poaching large, whole fish: make a generous and loose-fitting parcel of foil around the fish, pour in the poaching liquid, seal, place on a baking tray and poach in the oven.

Or, cut the fish in half, wrap in muslin or foil and poach, then rejoin the halves on the serving dish – disguise the join with a garnish or a sauce.

PERFECT POACHING

1. Place the fish in WARM poaching liquid, which should just cover the fish, and put on a gentle heat. Bring slowly up to barely simmering.
2. Continue to poach for 10-15 minutes for fillets, depending on the size and thickness of the fillet. Poach whole fish for approximately 8-10 minutes per 450 g (1 lb), if the fish is to be served hot.
3. For whole fish or cutlets to be served cold, cook for the same lengths of time given above, but allow the fish to cool in the poaching liquid. This retains the maximum flavour and moisture in the flesh.
4. You can incorporate the poaching liquid in an accompanying sauce.

BAKING AND ROASTING

The advantage of baking whole fish is that, with the addition of seasoning and herbs, the fish will cook beautifully in its own juices. To bake whole fish successfully, uncovered, stuffing is recommended to keep the fish moist, and it is a good idea to baste the fish fairly frequently. You can also wrap the fish in lightly greased foil, or in a paper parcel (en papillote). With either of these two methods, to help retain and add to the cooking juices, you can marinate the fish before cooking. I like to brush baked fish with a little oil, melted butter, or plain unsweetened yogurt and spices. Whole fish, or fillets can be baked on top of a bed of vegetables, such as sliced tomatoes, onions, garlic, mushrooms, carrots and chopped celery and slightly moistened with a dash of stock, wine, cider, cream or plain unsweetened yogurt.

PERFECT BAKING AND ROASTING

1. Always preheat the oven.
2. Do not overcook. Test that the fish is ready by inserting a skewer, or sharp pointed knife, into the thickest part of the fish – the flesh should ease off the bone and be opaque.
3. If not parcelled in foil, baste frequently.
4. Serve with its own cooking juices, or incorporate them in a sauce.

STEAMING

Steaming is particularly suitable for fish as it has the great advantage that the fish never comes into contact with the water but cooks gently in its own juices.

The fish can be wrapped in paper or foil parcels, having first been lightly seasoned and sprinkled with lemon juice or a drop of wine. The parcels of fish (which can be marinated first if you like) can also contain thinly sliced vegetables, such as spring onions and slices of fresh root ginger sprinkled with soy sauce (which is a standard Chinese derivation), leeks, or freshly chopped green herbs.

A conventional steamer can be used, the steamer rack in a wok, a Chinese bamboo steamer, or simply place the fish between two plates over a pan of boiling water.

PERFECT STEAMING

1. The fish must never come into contact with the water.
2. Keep the water in the steamer or pan boiling. If you have to add more water, use boiling, not cold, water.
3. Test that the fish is cooked by inserting a skewer or a sharp pointed knife into the fish – the flesh should ease off the bone and be opaque. Try not to overcook the fish.
4. Reserve the juices from the steamed fish to be incorporated in a sauce or simply poured over the fish when served.

GRILLING AND BARBECUING

White fish needs basting while it is cooking under the heat of the grill or over the barbecue. It can be marinated first for extra flavour and to protect its delicate and tender flesh. The skin of oily fish will protect the fish better and retain the moisture of the flesh. Remember to oil the grilling rack lightly. Sardines and small herring or mackerel can be grilled very quickly just as they are, but with large, whole fish make 2 or 3 slashes along the back to allow the heat to penetrate.

Sizzling fish, cooking over the barbecue, produces wonderful aromas. The same rules for grilling apply to barbecuing, bearing in mind that you must wait for the charcoal to be hot, and burned to a grey colour or, if using wood, wait for the flames to die down to glowing embers. Aromatic herbs can be thrown on the fire to enhance the flavour of the food. Fish can also be parcelled in foil and barbecued over the fire or pushed into the embers.

When grilling or barbecuing fish kebabs, oil the skewers first to prevent the flesh from sticking, and turn slowly for even cooking, basting frequently.

PERFECT GRILLING AND BARBECUING

1. Always preheat the grill, or light the barbecue in advance.
2. Fish should be grilled about 10 cm (4 inches) above or below the heat.
3. When grilling white fish, baste or brush frequently to prevent the flesh drying out. Melted butter, oil or an oil-based marinade can be used for basting.
4. Grill fish at the last moment and serve immediately.

BRAISING

Braising is a method of cooking fish which falls between baking and stewing, and where the flavour of the vegetables absorbs the flavour of the fish – and vice versa. Braising produces gently cooked and rather comforting fish dishes, and the vegetables, herbs and braising liquid can be served as part of the final dish. A combination of different fish is ideal for this method of cooking – you could try mixing smoked and white fish together, for instance – or taking advantage of the best buys at your fishmonger's. Left-overs from a braise can be used to make soups, or sauces for pasta.

The thick chunks of fish steaks should be placed on top of a mixture of sliced vegetables, fresh herbs and seasoned with salt and pepper, then water, wine or stock should be added. The dish should be covered with a lid or foil and baked in a moderate to moderately hot oven or simmered on top of the oven.

PERFECT BRAISING

1. The lid of the cooking dish should fit tightly to prevent evaporation – or you could use a double thickness of foil.
2. The dish must be cooked slowly to allow the exchange of flavours.
3. Serve all the vegetables and juices from the pan with the fish – or use the juices to flavour accompanying sauces.

FRYING

Frying is probably the most traditional British way of cooking fish. In recent years there has been concern that deep frying is not a very healthy method of cooking. However, if done properly, very little fat is absorbed while deep frying as long as the fat is at the right temperature. The blanket term of frying does include some of the quickest and most delicious ways to cook fish, if certain rules are followed.

Stir-frying is a good example of a brisk and healthy way to cook fish. You do not necessarily need a wok – although the even heat distribution in the shape of the shallow bowl is ideal for quick cooking – a large, shallow heavy frying pan will do. This method is suitable only for small pieces of fish, and you can stir-fry strips or chunks of fish (such as monkfish) or shellfish (such as prawns or scallops) with a combination of finely chopped vegetables. A good quality oil, such as sunflower or safflower should be used – avoid lard. Preparation for stir-frying must be done before you heat the wok or pan because it is a very quick cooking method. Stir-fry a small quantity of fish at a time, keeping it warm on a plate covered with paper towels to drain off any excess oil.

Sautéing or shallow frying is similar in theory to stir-frying. It is best done in a mixture of butter and oil, as the oil prevents the butter from burning. The fish should be dried before cooking or its dampness will cause a layer of steam which will prevent the fish from browning. The fish can be first dipped in milk or beaten egg and rolled lightly in seasoned flour or breadcrumbs.

Sauté a small quantity of fish pieces at a time – transferring them to a plate with a double piece of paper towel on it to absorb any remaining cooking fat.

Shake the pan around all the time while cooking so that the fish literally jumps around in the hot oil and butter.

To shallow fry fillets or steaks of fish, coat the fish with a dusting of seasoned flour or egg and breadcrumbs to protect the fish and seal in the flavour. The pan and fat must be hot before the fish is added then, when the fish is browned, reduce the heat and fry until tender.

Deep frying in well-used fat is bad news. Fish coated in batter should be deep fried in good, hot, clean oil.

For deep frying, the oil must be brought to the correct temperature (when it is shimmering with heat drop a cube of bread in – it should float straight to the surface and brown immediately). The ideal temperature is 190°C (375°F). When you deep fry fish at the correct temperature, a crust forms on the outside immediately so that hardly any oil is absorbed, and the moisture of the tender flesh is retained.

PERFECT FRYING

1. Always use good quality clean oil, for frying and stir-frying, or a mixture of oil and butter for sautéing.
2. All fish (or shellfish) needs a protective coating of flour, breadcrumbs or batter before being deep fried.
3. Drain fried food well on paper towels, and serve immediately.
4. In general, fried fish should not be served with rich sauces – wedges of lemon or a sharp tangy dressing are the most suitable accompaniments.
5. Remember that frying, especially deep frying, is a potentially dangerous method of cooking. Do not overfill pans with hot oil, and whilst cooking never leave the frying pan unattended.

MICROWAVE COOKING OF FISH

An advantage of cooking fish in a microwave is that, as there is little or no contact with water and the process of cooking is very quick, the vitamin, mineral and protein content is retained. The microwave is also good for quick defrosting and reheating of cooked dishes.

Remember, though, that you must adapt the cooking times to the model of microwave that you own. The timer control is important as microwave cooking is judged by time and power output.

Many basic cooking rules and methods apply when using the microwave, and cooking times and power levels will be given in your manufacturer's instruction book.

The cooking of fish in a microwave is based along the lines of baking, poaching and steaming, but bear in mind the following points. Extra moisture can increase cooking times as the microwaves interact mainly with water molecules. You will have to reduce the amount of liquid used for good results, but always cook and leave fish to stand for the recommended times to ensure that the fish is thoroughly cooked. Remember that fish continues to cook during standing time, after its removal from the oven. Finally, always cook the fish in a non-metallic container.

Fish can be shallow fried in a microwave by using a browning dish – but *deep frying* is not possible as it is difficult to control the oil temperature.

When cooking whole fish, lightly score the skin at the thickest parts to allow the steam to escape and wrap a *small* piece of foil around the tail to prevent it overcooking – don't let the foil touch the sides of the microwave. Tuck under the thin tail end of fillets to prevent overcooking.

PREPARING SEAFOOD

SCALING FISH

This is a job which your fishmonger should be happy to do for you when asked, but is also simple to do at home.

Although it is rather a messy job, and fish scales do tend to fly around somewhat! Therefore, first cover your work surface with newspaper.

You can buy a fish scaler quite cheaply to do this job, but using the blunt side of a sturdy knife is quite satisfactory.

REMOVING THE HEAD

Remove the head of the fish behind the gills using a sharp knife, then wash thoroughly. If leaving the head on it is necessary to remove the gills as they give a slightly bitter taste.

Lay the fish on newspaper on your working surface. Hold the tail with one hand and with the blunt side of a strong knife draw the knife from the tail end to the head end (i.e against the flow of the scales).

Wash the fish under cold running water, over a colander to catch the scales. Turn the fish on to its other side and repeat the process. Wash the fish and pat dry with paper towels. Be careful not to let the scales block up the sink.

CLEANING FISH

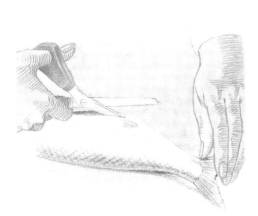

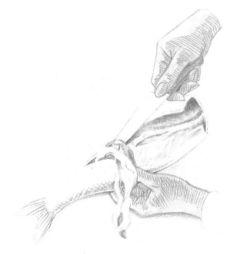

Place the fish on its back with the belly facing upwards. Using scissors or a sharp knife cut down the belly of the fish.

Remove the innards from the fish using a small sharp knife. Wash thoroughly under cold running water.

To clean a fish through the gills prise back the gill and, with your other finger and thumb, snap out the gill and pull out all the innards. Wash thoroughly.

FILLETING A ROUND FISH

Lay the clean fish on a chopping board, with its tail and back towards you. Hold the fish steady with one hand and make a semi-circular cut around the head (follow the bone structure and keep close to the head area). Slice along the backbone from head to tail. You should be able to feel the backbone as you keep the knife on top of it while slicing. Beginners can lift the fillet up as they go to see what they are doing.

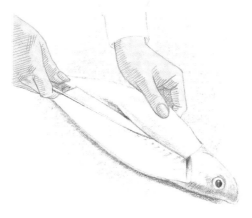

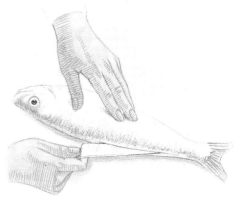

Lift the flesh gently and cut the fillet away from the body, taking care to avoid the 'rib' bones.

To remove the lower fillet, turn the fish over and repeat the process. Now you have the two fillets, trim them neatly ready for cooking.

BONING A ROUND FISH

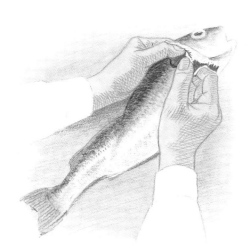

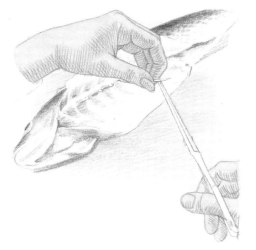

This is the method for boning a whole fish ready for stuffing. Clean the fish as described previously. Remove the gills (these can give a bitter taste when fish are cooked whole). Trim away the fins.

Lengthen the opening along the belly and expose the backbone and ribs. You can see the ribs in the flesh of the fish. Work down the backbone of the fish, freeing each rib with the aid of scissors and your fingers. Each rib can then be snapped off the backbone.

Now run a sharp knife down each side of the backbone. Using kitchen scissors or game shears, cut through the backbone at the head end of the fish and pull out the backbone, working towards the tail where you cut it free.

FILLETING A FLAT FISH

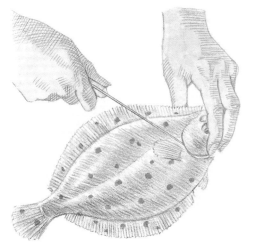

Place the fish on a chopping board with the head pointing towards you. To cut the head off, follow the 'shape' of the head with your knife, making sure you leave all the flesh and just remove the bony head.

You can feel and see the line of the backbone on the white side of the fish down the centre. Cut a line down the backbone and then insert your filleting knife into the flesh, and feel the tip resting against the backbone and on top of the 'rib' bones.

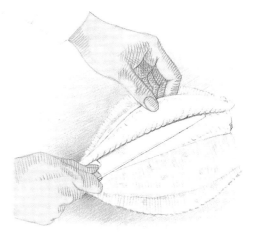

Slide the knife right down the backbone, then work with long, slicing motions across the ribs to the outer edge of the fish. Lift up the fillet, remove, and trim. Repeat on the other side – then turn over and remove the other two fillets.

SKINNING FISH

Lovers of fish have personal preferences about whether or not, or how, to skin fish. Many feel that if you leave the skin on it adds to the flavour of the fish, helps to keep its shape, and looks attractive when served. However, there are many recipes which call for skinned fish and, of course, your fishmonger will be able to help you out.

Large, whole round fish, if they are to be served cold, such as salmon, trout, and grey mullet, can be skinned after cooking, which is a very simple operation.

SKINNING FILLETS OF FLAT OR ROUND FISH

When skinning fish fillets, fingers dipped in salt will help you keep a grip on the skin.

Place the fillet, skin side down, on a chopping board, tail towards you. Make a 1 cm (½ inch) snip into the flesh at the tail end, then insert your knife. Holding the tail skin in one hand, work the knife in a sawing action, slicing the flesh away from the skin. Hold the knife at an acute angle (almost parallel) to the fish to avoid cutting the skin. Keep the skin taut, and stop once or twice to fold back the fillet so that you can see how you are going. The skin can be kept for stock.

SKINNING A WHOLE FLAT FISH

This is difficult to do, therefore it is worth attempting only on large fish such as Dover sole.

Remember to dip your fingers in salt to get a firm grip. Place the fish, skin side up, on a chopping board. Hold the tail in one hand and, with a sharp knife, cut into the skin at the tail end until you have a good flap to get a grasp on. With a very strong and firm motion, pull the skin towards the head. When you reach the jaws, turn the fish over – hold the fish by the head, and continue pulling the skin until you reach the tail.

EXTRACTING THE MEAT FROM A COOKED CRAB

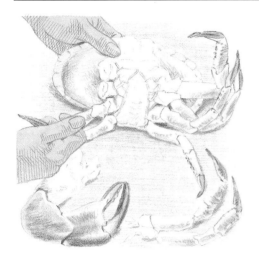

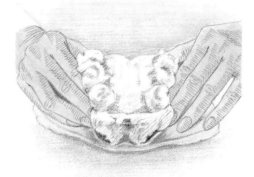

Twist off the main claws and legs from the body of the crab: they come away easily. As the meat is fiddly to extract from the little legs you could pound them and boil them for stock or soup. To crack the main claws, cup the largest joint in the palm of your hand, and smack it smartly with a wooden rolling pin or mallet.

Using your fingers, remove the white flesh from the main claws. There is a flat bone (which feels and looks rather like the end of a plastic spatula) to remove from part of the white claw meat. The handle of a teaspoon is useful for scooping out the flesh of the two other joints broken off from the main claws.

Put the body of the crab on a chopping board with the head facing away from you. Push the 'undercarriage' with your thumbs and prise away the underside of the crab so that it comes clean out of the shell. It is very important to remove the soft feathery gills (dead men's or devil's fingers) and the stomach sac (found directly behind the mouth part) as these are not edible.

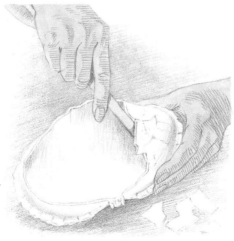

With a heavy sharp knife, cut the underbody in half lengthways and pick out the white meat and creamy brown meat. The brown meat in the shell may be rather watery, so shake out the water and check that the colour of the meat is pink to brown and healthy looking. Scoop out with a teaspoon. For dressed crab, keep the brown meat separate.

If the shell is to be used for dressed or devilled crab, tap out the shell inside of the groove around the shell, which is clearly marked, with the handle of a wooden spoon or the tip of a rolling pin. Scrub clean with boiling soapy water before use and oil it lightly.

MUSSELS

Mussels have to be absolutely fresh when cooked. Buy the mussels from a reliable source, such as a fishmonger. If you have gathered them yourself, make sure that the area from which you have collected them is unpolluted. Before cooking, place these mussels in clean, salted water and leave overnight. It is important to remember to discard any dead mussels: they must be alive when cooked. Throw away any which do not close when tapped lightly.

Scrub the mussels well before cooking. Remove the tuft of hair-like strands from the mussel, known as the 'beard', by pulling away or cutting off with scissors.

EXTRACTING THE MEAT FROM A COOKED LOBSTER

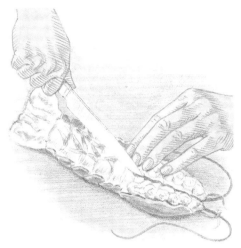

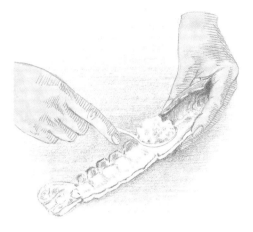

Lay the lobster on its back on a chopping board, twist off the main claws and legs and extract the white meat as for the crab.

If you are going to use the halved shells for a cooked lobster dish, or to serve a cold lobster salad, pull back the tail to extend the lobster, lay it on its back and, with a sharp heavy knife, cut down the middle and along the length of the lobster. You may need to give the knife a few sharp taps with a mallet. The white meat is now easily extracted from the tail.

With a teaspoon, scoop out the brown meat from the main shell and head. Remember to discard the white feathery gills (dead men's fingers). Remove the easily recognizable small stomach sac situated in the head, and also remove the grey-black thread of intestine running along into the tail. Scrub the shell clean with boiling soapy water before use.

SCALLOPS AND QUEENS

You can also buy these ready prepared, presented on their shells. Live scallops are also available and must be very fresh. This is the method for opening the shells, and preparing them.

Opening the shells: they can be difficult to separate. One solution is to place them, flat side down, on the top of a hot cooker for a few moments. This should make them gape slightly, and you can then use a stubby, stout knife to prise them open.

Then run the blade of a sharp knife along the inside of the upper (rounded) shell and lower (flat) shell to release the membrane of the scallop from the shells.

Now rinse the scallop under cold running water, and use your fingers or a small knife to remove the membrane from the white lobe and pink coral and free them from the shell. Discard the greyish fringy skirt if you wish – although this is edible and good for the stock pan.

Trim away any unwanted matter from the flesh on a chopping board. The rounded shell can be scrubbed in boiling water and used either as a container for a cold dish or lightly oiled to hold a baked or grilled dish.

OPENING OYSTERS

Opening is usually known as 'shucking' an oyster. This is not easy for the beginner – but it gets easier as you go along.

Take a teatowel in one hand to help you get a grip. Grasp the oyster firmly, making sure it lies flat side up in your palm. Insert the blade of a round short-bladed, stout knife or oyster knife into the hinge of the oyster and prise open.

As you are separating the shells, slide in a sharp knife and cut the oyster free from the top and bottom of the shells. Take care to keep in the juice and remove any flakes of shell that may have fallen on top of the oyster. The oyster is now ready to serve.

FISH STOCK

MAKES 1.2 litres (2 pints)

*750 g (1½ lb) bones and trimmings from
white fish
900 ml (1½ pints) water
1 onion, peeled and sliced
1 carrot, peeled and chopped
1 leek, trimmed and chopped
300 ml (½ pint) white wine or cider
6 black peppercorns, bruised
1 bouquet garni (including thyme, sage,
tarragon and bay leaf)*

Ask your fishmonger for bones from fish
such as turbot or Dover sole, if possible or
use a whole inexpensive fish like whiting
for a really tasty stock. Do not use oily fish.

1. Put everything except the peppercorns
into a large saucepan, bring to the boil,
and simmer for 30 minutes, skimming off
any scum that rises to the surface from
time to time.
2. Add the peppercorns for the last
10 minutes of cooking time.

MILK, LEMON AND HERB STOCK

MAKES 600 ml (1 pint)

*300 ml (½ pint) milk
300 ml (½ pint) water
2-3 lemons, peeled and sliced
1 bouquet garni*

This is good for poaching fish and needs
no preliminary cooking – it can be used
when the fish is removed to make a sauce
or flavour a dressing.

1. Poach the fish in this mixture but do not
allow it to boil.
2. Transfer the fish to a heated serving
dish and use the stock as required.

COURT BOUILLON

MAKES 1.5 litres (2½ pints)

*1.2 litres (2 pints) water
225 g (8 oz) carrots, peeled and chopped
2 medium onions, peeled and sliced
1 stick celery, trimmed and chopped
1 bouquet garni (parsley, bay leaf and
thyme)
6 black peppercorns, bruised
300 ml (½ pint) white wine*

Court bouillon is the term used for a
flavoured stock which can be made into a
sauce, soup or stew, or in which fish or
shellfish can be cooked.

1. Put all the ingredients into a large saucepan and bring to the boil.
2. Simmer for 1 hour, strain and leave
to cool.

BASIC WHITE SAUCE

MAKES 600 ml (1 pint)

*50 g (2 oz) plain flour
50 g (2 oz) butter or margarine
600 ml (1 pint) milk
salt
freshly ground black pepper*

1. In a heavy based saucepan, melt the
butter, add the flour and stir continuously
for 2 minutes over a low heat.
2. Gradually add the milk, off the heat,
stirring all the time. Cook the sauce over a
low heat for 2-3 minutes until the sauce
thickens. Season to taste with salt and
pepper.

Variations:
Parsley Sauce: Towards the end of cooking the sauce, add a good 2 tablespoons of
finely chopped parsley and a squeeze of
fresh lemon juice.

Mornay Sauce: Add 75-100 g (3-4 oz)
grated Gruyère or Cheddar cheese. Alternatively, use 25 g (1 oz) freshly grated
Parmesan together with 50 g (2 oz) grated
Gruyère or Cheddar cheese. Stir into the
sauce as it is thickening and continue stirring until all the cheese is melted and the
sauce is smooth. Add 1 teaspoon prepared
English mustard if desired.
Mushroom Sauce: Gently cook 100 g
(4 oz) sliced button mushrooms in a little
butter or oil – do not let them brown. Add
to the sauce in the finishing stage, with a
pinch of cayenne.

BECHAMEL SAUCE

MAKES 600 ml (1 pint)

*600 ml (1 pint) milk
1 bay leaf
6 black peppercorns
½ small onion or 1 shallot, peeled and finely
sliced
40 g (1½ oz) butter or margarine
50 g (2 oz) plain flour
salt
single cream (optional)*

This béchamel is well worth taking a little
trouble over for a 'special effort' sauce.

1. Put the milk in a pan over a low heat,
add the bay leaf, peppercorns and onion
and infuse for about 8 minutes. Do not let
the milk boil.
2. Melt the butter in a heavy based
saucepan and stir in the flour. Cook for
1-2 minutes on a low heat.
3. Remove from the heat and stir in the
strained warm milk, whisking all the time
to keep it smooth.
4. Just simmer the sauce on a low heat for
1-2 minutes until the sauce thickens, taste
and adjust the seasoning if necessary. A
little single cream can be added at this
point, if desired.

SAFFRON SAUCE

MAKES about 150 ml (¼ pint)

1 small onion or 2 shallots, peeled
150 ml (¼ pint) dry white wine
150 ml (¼ pint) double cream
pinch of saffron powder

1. Finely chop the onion or shallots and place in a saucepan with the wine. Bring to the boil and simmer until the wine is reduced to about 1 tablespoon.
2. Remove from the heat, stir in the cream and saffron powder.

HOLLANDAISE SAUCE

MAKES 300 ml (½ pint)

3 tablespoons white wine vinegar
2 tablespoons water
6 white peppercorns
100-175 g (4-6 oz) butter
3 egg yolks
squeeze of fresh lemon juice
salt

Hollandaise sauce is not thickened by flour but uses the reduction method to concentrate flavour and is thickened with eggs and butter. It is served warm rather than hot, and takes a little patience and time to prepare, though the end result is well worth it.

1. Put the vinegar, water and peppercorns into a small, heavy based saucepan, bring to the boil and reduce the liquid to about 1 tablespoon.
2. Strain the vinegar mixture into a bowl and leave to cool.
3. Meanwhile, melt the butter. Beat the egg yolks until frothy. Stand the bowl of vinegar over a pan of simmering water (making sure that the bowl does not touch the water), and beat in the egg yolk. Then,

very gradually, add three quarters of the melted butter, drop by drop, beating all the time until the sauce thickens and is of a creamy consistency.
4. Add a squeeze of lemon juice and, if the sauce is too sharp, add a little of the reserved melted butter. If the mixture thickens too quickly as you are cooking, remove it before returning to the heat and continuing to beat.

FRESH TOMATO SAUCE

MAKES 600 ml (1 pint)

1 medium onion, peeled and finely chopped
1 clove garlic, crushed (optional)
2 teaspoons olive oil
1 medium carrot, peeled and grated
750 g (1½ lb) ripe tomatoes
1 teaspoon tomato purée
1 tablespoon chopped fresh herbs, such as
  basil, tarragon or oregano
salt
freshly ground black pepper
a little red or white wine (optional)

This sauce is extremely versatile, you can add more, or less, herbs of your own choice to suit the recipe you are cooking. The carrot adds a little sweetness and colour to the sauce so do include it!

1. Gently cook the onion and garlic in the olive oil until softened. Add the carrot and cook for another 1-2 minutes.
2. Peel the tomatoes and chop coarsely. Add these and all the other ingredients to the pan. Bring up to just simmering point and cook for about 10 minutes. Blend until smooth.
3. Cook for a longer time to reduce and thicken if you need this sauce to add to another sauce dish. Add a little red or white wine if you desire.

MAYONNAISE

MAKES about 300 ml (½ pint)

2 egg yolks
½ teaspoon Dijon mustard
300 ml (½ pint) olive or sunflower oil
1-2 tablespoons white wine vinegar
salt
white pepper
pinch of cayenne (optional)
squeeze of fresh lemon juice

A lot has been made of the method and mystique of making mayonnaise by hand, and yet if all the ingredients are at room temperature, the eggs are more than three days old, and the mixing bowl is perfectly dry, you should not have any problem!

1. Put the egg yolks and mustard into a small mixing bowl (I like to stand the bowl on a damp dish-cloth or teatowel to stop it slipping around while beating and adding the oil). Beat with a small wooden spoon until the yolks are creamy.
2. As you are beating, stir in the oil drop by drop, increasing to a steady trickle as the mayonnaise thickens.
3. Keep beating all the time. (If the mayonnaise separates, take another egg yolk and beat it in another basin, then slowly add to the separated mixture, beating all the time, until it thickens and becomes smooth again.)
4. When all the oil has been incorporated, add the vinegar – the mayonnaise will lighten in colour immediately. Season with salt and pepper, add a pinch of cayenne, if desired, and a squeeze of lemon juice.

Variation:
Cocktail Sauce: Add 1 tablespoon tomato purée, a dash of Tabasco sauce and a squeeze of lemon juice to 150 ml (¼ pint) mayonnaise. Season to taste with salt and pepper.

AIOLI

MAKES 300 ml (½ pint)

6 garlic cloves
salt
freshly ground black pepper
2 egg yolks
300 ml (½ pint) olive oil
squeeze of fresh lemon juice

This is the famous garlic mayonnaise of Provençe. You can use a little less garlic according to your taste.

1. Peel the garlic cloves, and pound them in a basin, with a pinch of salt, until they are thoroughly mashed.
2. Add the egg yolks and beat with a wooden spoon.
3. Add the oil drop by drop, beating all the time and continue until the sauce thickens and all the oil is incorporated. When the mixture is creamy, add lemon juice and pepper to taste.

WATERCRESS SAUCE

MAKES 900 ml (1½ pints)

2-3 bunches watercress
900 ml (1½ pints) water
salt
squeeze of fresh lemon juice
2 tablespoons fromage blanc or low-fat
  cream cheese

1. Wash and trim the watercress and cook in boiling salted water for 2 minutes.
2. Drain well and plunge into cold water, then drain again.
3. Put the watercress into the bowl of a food processor and purée until smooth. Then add the fromage blanc or cream cheese and process until smooth. You can gently re-heat this sauce or serve it chilled.

VINAIGRETTE DRESSING

3 tablespoons olive or sunflower oil
1 tablespoon white wine vinegar
½ teaspoon Dijon mustard
salt
freshly ground black pepper

1. Put all the ingredients together in a screw-top jar and shake vigorously to combine.

Variations:
Lemon Dressing: Substitute 1 tablespoon lemon juice for the vinegar.
Herb Dressing: Add 1 tablespoon chopped fresh herbs to the dressing.
Garlic Dressing: Add 1-2 crushed garlic cloves to the dressing.

SAVOURY BUTTERS

Take a freshly grilled, poached or baked fish and add a slice of savoury butter and you will have a succulent and delectable fish dish. Use only a tiny knob of butter for flavouring white fish (it is unnecessary for oily fish). However, the fish should not be served swimming in melted butter.

MAITRE D'HOTEL BUTTER

100 g (4 oz) unsalted butter, softened
2 tablespoons finely chopped fresh parsley
½ teaspoon lemon juice
salt
freshly ground black pepper

1. Beat the butter until creamy, then add the chopped parsley, lemon juice and season with salt and pepper to taste.
2. Shape into a roll in greaseproof paper, then twist the ends tightly.
3. Chill and cut slices as required.

Variations:
Lemon Butter: Add 1 teaspoon freshly grated lemon rind plus a squeeze of fresh lemon juice, to the softened butter. Use the same method to make Lime Butter.
Herb Butter: Add 2 tablespoons finely chopped fresh herbs to the butter.
Mint Butter: Add 2 tablespoons chopped fresh mint to the softened butter.
Garlic Butter: Beat 2 cloves crushed garlic and 2 teaspoons snipped chives into the butter.
Tomato Butter: Add 2 tablespoons tomato purée or fresh tomato pulp to the softened butter. Squeeze in some fresh lemon juice and season with a pinch of freshly ground black pepper.
Anchovy Butter: Pound 4-6 anchovy fillets to a smooth paste and beat this, or a few drops of anchovy sauce, into the butter. This is very good spread on water biscuits or toast and baked until crisp.

INDEX

ACKNOWLEDGEMENTS

Photographer
NICK CARMAN

Photographic styling
MARIAN PRICE

Preparation of food for photography
JANICE MURFITT

Illustrations
CLAIRE ATTRIDGE

Step-by-step illustrations
PATRICIA CAPON

Cover photograph
VERNON MORGAN

Preparation of food for cover photograph
KATHY MAN